THE
ADVENTURE
of BEING a WIFE

THE ADVENTURE  of BEING a WIFE

by Mrs. Norman Vincent Peale

PRENTICE-HALL, INC.
ENGLEWOOD CLIFFS, NEW JERSEY

The Adventure of Being a Wife
by Mrs. Norman Vincent Peale

DEDICATED
TO MY HUSBAND

Norman Vincent Peale

WHO MADE IT POSSIBLE
FOR ME TO HAVE
THE ADVENTURE OF BEING A WIFE

With Appreciation
to

Arthur Gordon

Skilled Writer
for His Valued and
Understanding Assistance
in the Preparation of This Book

CONTENTS

have no intention of marrying him. He's not my first lover, and I'm sure he won't be the last. But what's wrong with this? Perhaps someday I'll decide I want children, in which case the pressures of society will probably make marriage seem advisable. But until then I want no part of it. And even then I don't intend to be trapped in it if it goes badly." She shook back her dark hair in a defiant gesture. "We're not blind, Mrs. Peale. We look around and we see what marriage does to people and we don't like what we see. I think when I say these things I'm speaking for a large part of my generation. Do you have any answer?"

All the bright young faces swung in my direction, and I took a deep breath. It was true. I had said that in my opinion marriage was the greatest career a woman could have. I had agreed that a woman might have other stimulating and important jobs, but none was so difficult and demanding, so exciting and potentially rewarding as the job of living with a man, studying him, supporting him, liberating his strengths, compensating for his weaknesses, making his whole mechanism soar and sing the way it was designed to do. I had said this because I believed it completely, but I hadn't expected a challenge quite so blunt and harsh as this one. Modern marriage, this handsome young woman was saying, was a fraud and a mockery—and she wanted to know if I had an answer.

"Yes," I said to her quietly, "I have an answer, because I'm in the process of living it. I consider myself one of the most fortunate women alive. Why? Because I am totally married to a man in every sense of the word: physically, emotionally, intellectually, spiritually. We're so close that you couldn't put a knife blade between us. I need him and depend on him completely. He completely needs and depends on me. We're not two lonely, competing individuals. We're one integrated, mutually responsive, mutually supportive organism—and this is such a marvelous and joyous thing that nothing else in life can even approach it. It's the greatest of all adventures, but *you'll* never know it. You'll never even come within shouting distance of it if you maintain the attitudes and the code of conduct you've adopted."

"I don't see why not," she said, but her voice had lost some of its conviction. "Why can't a man-woman relationship be just as meaningful outside of marriage as in it?"

"Because," I told her, "it doesn't have the key ingredients. It doesn't have the commitment. It doesn't have the permanence. It can never achieve the depth that comes from total sharing, from working together toward common goals year after year, from knowing that you're playing the game for keeps. Do you think my husband and I have achieved the relationship we have just by thinking happy thoughts or waving a wand? Don't be absurd! We fought for this relationship! We hammered it out on the anvil of joy and sorrow, of pain and problems—yes, at times, of discouragement and disagreement. But we never thought of marriage as a trap. We thought of it as a privilege. And there's quite a difference!"

The dark-haired girl sat down, and a tall boy in blue jeans spoke up. "If marriage is all that good, Mrs. Peale," he said, "why is it that one out of four American marriages ends up on the rocks?"

"Any sociologist could give you a dozen fancy reasons," I told him. "I'll give you three quick ones.

"To begin with, a lot of people who get divorced quit too easily. They give up without a fight, because they don't know that what they have is worth fighting for. They give up because they've been allowed to think that everything will be moonlight and roses, when actually it isn't. They give up because unconsciously they've come into the marriage with an escape route already planned, via the divorce court, if everything isn't automatically just dandy. That's one reason why one out of every four marriages winds up on the rocks.

"Another reason is that the women involved aren't using

their heads. In this whole area of human relations, women are smarter than men. They ought to be able to study their man, figure out what his needs are, what makes him tick. They ought to help him know where he wants to go. They ought to be able to anticipate trouble and head it off. They ought to be brainy enough and sexy enough to hold a husband. But a lot of them are not, mainly because they're too lazy or too spoiled, or too busy thinking about themselves and what they're getting or not getting out of their marriages.

"And the third reason is that too many people go around downgrading marriage these days. It has become a favorite indoor sport. The result is that wherever I go young married women come up to me and bewail their fate. They've been brainwashed into thinking that they're caught in an unrewarding, unstimulating, unchallenging, drab existence. Sometimes I feel like taking them by the shoulders and shaking them. 'Wake up!' I want to tell them, 'Get with it! Here you are, right in the middle of the most fascinating role a woman can play and you don't even know it!'

"You just heard your classmate say that your generation has looked at marriage and doesn't like what it sees. Well, my answer is that your generation hasn't looked very far— or else is seeing only what it wants to see! This country is full of good marriages, built by men and women who know that good marriages don't just happen, they have to be *made* to happen; that it takes more brains and determination than some people are willing to invest; that you have to work at it twenty-four hours a day; that the job is never finished. But when you do, the dividends are enormous. Just enormous!"

Outside in the corridor a bell rang, and I paused, a little out of breath.

"Well," said my professor friend who was conducting the seminar, "that's all for today. Interesting and stimulating, I think. Class dismissed."

The students filed out, some thanking me pleasantly for

being with them. One lingered behind, a girl with red hair, not pretty, but with a good-humored, lively face. "Mrs. Peale," she said earnestly, "why don't you make an effort to say to other people what you've been saying to us? I mean, lots of people, not just a handful of students. I think it needs to be said loud and clear. You're obviously so happy in your own marriage, and have made such a success of it, that you ought to tell everyone how you did it and how they can do it."

"I do talk about it," I said, "whenever I get a chance. At church meetings, or at groups like this one, or even now and then on radio or television interviews."

"That's fine," she said, "but the audience is too limited. Besides, people forget what they hear very quickly. You spoke of the adventure of being a wife. Why don't you write a book about your own experiences in marriage? A book that people could read and refer to over and over? You could even call it 'The Adventure of Being a Wife.' "

"I wish I could," I said with a smile. "But in the first place I don't have literary skill or training. And in the second place, I don't know where I'd find the time."

"Think about it anyway," she said. "Just think about it." And she was gone.

Well, I did think about it, all through the rest of the day. I thought about it when the woman I had lunch with told me that her daughter, a fine young woman with two small children, was getting a divorce. Why? Because she and her husband had decided they weren't suited to each other. "Ruth," my friend said sadly, "I just don't understand it. In the past, when a marriage fell apart, there was usually some well-defined reason: infidelity, or cruelty, or alcoholism, or *something*. But now the virus that causes marriages to collapse seems to be affecting people who used to be considered almost immune: decent people, churchgoing people, intelligent people, and educated people."

I thought about that unhappy woman and her daughter and her two innocent grandchildren as I rode a Manhattan bus down to the corner of Fifth Avenue and 29th Street where the Marble Collegiate Church stands, its slender spire sharp against the sky. My husband, Norman, has been pastor of that church since 1932; in the past four decades I've heard him preach hundreds of sermons from its pulpit. It's a grand old church with a history going back to 1628—actually it's the oldest institution in New York—and I love it, not only for its great tradition, but for the way it keeps up with the times.

About a year ago, for example, it inaugurated a service known as Help Line, a battery of telephones manned by experts in human relations, most of them volunteers, who answer calls from distressed or troubled people. In its first six months of operations, the Help Line handled 34,032 such calls, many routine, but some highly dramatic. During my brief visit to the church on this particular day I happened to meet one of the directors of Help Line. "Tell me," I asked him, "what percentage of Help Line calls have to do with marriage problems?"

He thought for a moment. "Too many," he said thoughtfully. "If you include problems like alcoholism or drug addiction that are having a detrimental effect on the caller's marriage, then I'd say the proportion of marriage-problem calls is very high. Why do you ask?"

I told him about my morning at the university and also what my luncheon companion had said. "It left me wondering about the state of modern marriage," I said. "Why is it so shaky? Why are there so many break-ups? Do you have any theory?"

He wrinkled his forehead thoughtfully. "I don't know," he said. "Sometimes it just seems to me that it's a question of pressure. Modern living is so complex. Things happen so fast that sometimes the centrifugal forces in a marriage get the upper hand, and when that happens the marriage begins to break up or fly apart."

The centrifugal forces in marriage . . . that phrase kept coming back to me as, late in the afternoon, I drove up to Pawling, New York, to join Norman in our old white farmhouse high up on the ridge known as Quaker Hill. A question kept nagging at me: Was there anything that I could do, or say, or write, that might tend to counteract those destructive forces? It seemed presumptuous to think that there might be. And yet . . .

I didn't mention the matter to Norman until I had finished the supper dishes (the only "help" at the Hill Farm, most of the time, is myself!) and we were sitting on the porch, watching the April twilight sift down through the stately maples and the shadows gather in the folds of the Catskills across the valley. Then I told him about my day, about the seminar, about the challenge the dark-haired girl had flung at me and the suggestion the red-headed girl had made. "I know it sounds silly," I said. "I've never tried to write a book. But it was odd how the subject of marriage kept cropping up, wherever I went, whatever I did, all day long."

"Maybe it's not so silly," Norman said. "Maybe you're supposed to do something about all this."

We were both silent for a while. "You know," Norman said finally, "I think an upbeat, optimistic book about marriage might help a lot of people and do a lot of good. You don't have to be very perceptive nowadays to know that we're living in a deeply disturbed world and a terribly troubled nation. Things have changed radically in the last ten or twelve years—and not for the better. One reason, almost certainly, is the state of the modern home, which is a reflection of the relationship called marriage. That's where attitudes and values are formed. If the home is solid, you have a solid society. If it's not, you have crime, divorce, riots, alcoholism, drug abuse . . . all the things that add up to anarchy."

"Are you thinking about some sort of marriage manual?" I asked him. "That would call for a real expert, wouldn't it?"

"I'm not thinking about a manual," he said. "I'm thinking about a book where you just talk informally about yourself, your marriage, and all the things that go into it. The things we do together. The people we see. The problems we try to solve for ourselves or for others. The trips we take. The arguments we sometimes have that you prefer to call discussions. Anything that comes to mind."

"But I'm not a writer," I protested. "What do I know about writing a book?"

"A lot," he said. "You've helped me with all of mine, every step of the way. You edit my sermons, my newspaper column, everything I write. As for your qualifications, you've had years of learning about marriage simply by living it. We've raised three children who—if I do say so myself—have all turned out well. Not a dropout or a drug addict in the bunch. Now they're all happily married. In addition, over the years, we've listened to hundreds of married couples with every conceivable kind of problem and tried to help them sort out the tangles. You've been as much a part of this as I have. We've done it face to face with troubled people. We've done it in talks and sermons. We've done it by mail, on the telephone, by radio, on television, in books and magazines, on trains and planes and ocean liners. I know you have a lot of valuable techniques and insights, because I've heard you use them."

"I suppose so," I said doubtfully.

"Look," my husband said, "you believe that marriage is a great challenge, a great opportunity, a great adventure. You want to get that message across. So how do you do it? You just tell how that adventure happened to you—to us. Let the reader see us as we really are, just struggling human beings with faults and virtues like everyone else. If you're honest, the reader will stick right with you and learn a lot."

"I don't see how I'd get any continuity into such a book," I said glumly. "It'd just be a collection of bits and pieces, like a . . . patchwork quilt."

"There's nothing wrong with a patchwork quilt," Norman said cheerfully, "if it's colorful and it keeps you warm."

"But where should I begin?"

"Where did you first start learning the things you want to talk about?"

I had to think about that for a minute. "I guess it was when I had my first job," I said finally, "behind that ribbon counter in the department store in Detroit."

"That's a fine place to start," Norman said. "Who could have a better springboard than a ribbon counter in a department store in Detroit?"

"Well," I said doubtfully, "maybe next week I'll try to start making a few notes."

"If you put this thing off," my husband said, "you'll never start. So you'd better set a specific time. Like tomorrow morning. At seven A.M."

"Seven A.M.!" I cried. "That's when I'm supposed to be making the coffee!"

"Seven A.M.," he said firmly. "I'll make the coffee."

"But suppose I find I can't do it?"

"You used to say you couldn't make a speech, remember? I told you that you could—and I was right. You said you couldn't preside over a public meeting. I told you that you could—and you did. Remember the phrase we've quoted to so many people: *Do the thing you fear, and the death of fear is certain.*"

"It may be the death of *me*," I said sadly.

"We'll risk it," said my heartless husband. "Go and set the alarm clock!"

🌿 2 🌿

SOMETHING
OF
MYSELF

🌿 The thing I remember most vividly about that
first job of mine was the department store customer who
gave me such a hard time. She was a sharp-faced woman
with bleached hair and a harsh voice, and I can see her
now as she pawed through my neatly arranged merchandise
at the ribbon counter, complaining, grumbling, criticizing,
finding nothing that pleased her—and being quite rude in
the process. When I applied for a summer job, I had been
told that so far as salespeople were concerned, the customer
was always right. It was hard to believe that such an impossible person as this could be right about anything. But I
held my tongue. I needed the job, even if it paid only $11
per week. I was fourteen. I wouldn't be fifteen until
September.

When the difficult customer finally moved on after a
small purchase, I drew a sigh of relief. As I began sorting
my tangled merchandise, I reviewed my performance and
even felt a little smug. I had remained calm and polite; I
had kept smiling—most of the time, anyway. And after all,
I told myself, such people were the exception, not the rule.

I had gotten the job on my own, partly to earn a little
spending money, partly to help out at home. My father, a
minister, was a man of great kindliness and dignity, but I

doubt if he ever earned more than $2,400 a year in his life. My mother, tiny and deeply devout, had a marked musical gift; she played the piano and sometimes gave music lessons that brought in a little extra cash. Both my brothers had paper routes; I remember very well that if one of them was sick, Mother and I would get up at five in the morning and walk the route for him, sometimes in freezing rain or deep snow, folding the papers as we went and tossing them onto porches of houses whose owners—fortunate souls—were still snug in bed. I didn't enjoy being a substitute paper-carrier. But delivering the papers was a family responsibility, and in our family that concept was never taken lightly.

My father, who had a strong sense of justice, thought that $11 per week was very little for the store to be paying me, even if I was only fourteen years old. He had advised me to ask for a raise, and (full of qualms) I had done so. The manager had told me that he would think it over and let me know. At closing time that day—the day made memorable by the difficult customer—he called me in and told me that my request was granted. Henceforth I would be paid $13 per week. "And do you know why?" he said. "We sent one of our shoppers to your counter this morning, a lady we use to check on the performance of our salespeople. We told her to be as difficult as possible—and to observe how you reacted. I'm glad to say you passed the test very well indeed."

I don't think my feet touched the ground all the way home. I rushed in and threw my arms around my mother. "I got it! I got it!" I cried, breathless with excitement, and poured out my story. When I told it again at the supper table, my father smiled. "You see," he said, "it pays to be patient and kind, no matter how unfair life may seem to be at the time."

It was a lesson far more valuable than the extra two dollars a week.

Lack of money was chronic in the Stafford family, but it

never seemed to bother us very much. It was a way of life, something we took for granted. Mother and I made most of our clothes. No matter where we lived, Father always found a piece of unused land or a vacant lot and got permission from the owner to start a vegetable garden. We had to skimp on meat—I don't remember ever having steak or a piece of rare roast beef until I was in college. But no one was ever hungry. Sometimes Mother would buy a can of salmon for fifteen cents and make a delicious meal— scalloped salmon—that fed the whole family. The other day I bought a similar can of salmon and winced when I looked at the price: $1.07!

My earliest recollection is the L-shaped porch of a small white house standing next to a church. Both my parents, born in Canada, were naturalized Americans.

During the early years of their marriage, my father moved from one small town to another, sometimes starting a church in a place that had none, sometimes building up one that had run down. I was born in Fonda, Iowa, on my parents' fifth wedding anniversary—Dad always said I was their "wooden-anniversary present." I was the second child in the family, and the only girl. My brother Charles—Chuck, we called him—was three years older. Two years after I was born my brother Bill came along, and the family was complete.

The small towns and parsonages of my early childhood are a blur in my mind. It wasn't until we moved to Detroit when I was seven or eight, and settled in a modest house on Clairmount Avenue, that things began to have a degree of permanence.

Looking back from the turmoil and tension that surround children of today, my own childhood seems like a happy, well-ordered dream. I loved to play jacks on the sidewalks or the porch steps; I was a fanatical rope-skipper. I walked to and from school, almost a mile, and never considered it a hardship. There were the usual childhood squabbles with my brothers, and being the only girl and in the middle at that, I felt they ganged up on me. But there were no real quarrels or clashes of temperament.

One faintly traumatic event I recall vividly was the occasion during World War I when some ultra-patriotic teacher asked all the children in the classroom who had bought a war bond to stand up. I was the only one, or almost the only one, to remain seated, and I can feel the humiliation to this day. After school, I ran home to my mother in tears. Why hadn't I bought a war bond? She told me the truth. Our family couldn't afford to buy war bonds. There never was enough money even for essentials. We always went without something. But she reminded me that we were doing our part, that she and I were constantly knitting socks and sweaters for the soldiers with wool or yarn supplied by the Red Cross. This was little consolation, although I knitted frantically from that time on. I still think that teacher was cruel and misguided—or at best very thoughtless.

There were some wonderful teachers, though, and I remember them with affection and gratitude. In high school there was Mrs. Watson, our homeroom teacher: white-haired, motherly, a good disciplinarian. I learned something about serenity and self-control just by watching her. Then there was Miss Getamy, demanding but encouraging, who taught public speaking—a rather surprising course to find in a public school in those days.

We had to make three-minute speeches at regular intervals. I can still see Miss Getamy sitting in the back of the classroom appraising each performance, encouraging us in a quiet way. Her practical suggestions, her constant insistence that we learn to think on our feet and not depend upon notes, her emphasis on thinking of the class as one person instead of a crowd, gave me an assurance before people that proved of great help in the years to come.

In my eyes she was always right. One day when I was wearing a green dress she said, "Ruth, you should never, never wear green." And she added, "It makes your eyes turn green." I was crushed. Green eyes! I didn't wear anything green for at least fifteen years. Then one day, looking longingly at a beautiful green dress in a store, I said to the salesgirl, "How lovely," and added wistfully, "but not for me. I can't wear green." "Why not?" the salesgirl asked. "Because," I said repeating Miss Getamy verbatim after a decade and a half, "it makes my eyes turn green."

"What's wrong with green eyes?" the salesgirl asked cheerfully. "Most people think they're distinctive and pretty."

I must have stared at her for half a minute, digesting this momentous news. "They do?" I said incredulously. With some misgiving I bought the dress and never enjoyed anything more! And I have always had a green dress in my wardrobe ever since.

But I still wonder, every time I wear green, if Miss Getamy is revolving gently in her grave.

With so little money available, an atmosphere of insecurity might easily have haunted our home. But it didn't. Both our parents were controlled, disciplined people. They trusted the Lord, but they also felt He expected them to deal with everyday problems prudently and without complaining. We never ran up bills in our house or lived on credit. If money was short, we ate more vegetables and cut out the few small luxuries we sometimes had. I thought everyone lived this way—at least, all pastors and their families. I remember how startled I was, years later, to learn that Norman's parents lived cheerfully and sometimes precariously on credit—and even ran up bills at the grocery store! Of course, as a pastor in larger churches, and then a District Superintendent in the Methodist church, Father Peale earned much more money than my father did. But to hear the Peales wondering audibly and sometimes with melodramatic lamentations how this bill or that one could be paid was a revelation—and one that made me a little nervous!

Once in a while my father would have to borrow from the bank simply to get by. I remember once when a note for $200 came due and he couldn't meet it. We had a family conference at which each of us children emptied out nickels and dimes from our piggy banks and piled them on the kitchen table. It all added up to about $25. Father took the money, made a partial payment on the loan, and got an extension. But our savings were all paid back later, to the penny.

All through these formative years, the sense of family solidarity and security was very strong. We children didn't have many material possessions, but we had the peace of mind and the room to grow that come from a balanced combination of love and discipline inside the home. We had a lot of fun with music. Some of Mother's talent was passed along to all of us, and we spent a lot of time around the piano, harmonizing favorite songs and hymns. We became, in time, quite an accomplished family singing group and gave concerts at churches; I still have some of those old programs with a photograph of the singing Staffords on them. These early public performances brought in no money—the collections always went to the church—but they gave us children a certain poise and self-assurance that were invaluable in later life.

Religion was a part of our life, but it was not a self-conscious or ultra-pious religion. It was something to be lived, not talked about at length. We said grace at meals. Sunday was a quiet day—no movies, no noisy games. From the start, my own faith seemed as natural as breathing. I never had any intellectual doubts to resolve or great internal conflicts. I simply believed the Christian story and message, and drew strength when I needed it from my prayers and my faith.

So those years passed—predictable, pleasant, secure. We had few pets; my mother didn't care for animals in the house. I never went to summer camp, or had access to things like horseback riding. But we had picnics in Detroit's Belle Isle Park, and "pound parties" where everyone brought a pound of this or that to the parsonage. My father and brothers were baseball fans, and once in a while would take me to watch the Tigers play at Briggs Stadium—always from the bleachers.

In the summer, sometimes, we took short vacation trips on Great Lakes steamers. These might last three or four days and were a great adventure. I still remember the great picnic hampers full of food that we took along. There was never enough money to go into the restaurant. Sometimes, usually in August, we would go up to Canada to visit my mother's parents in the tiny town of Markham, near Toronto. Grandfather Crosby was a retired carriage-maker; he and Grandmother Crosby were plain, good people whose parents had come from England. They were pillars of the local Methodist church. Their house had neither electricity nor running water, but we city children had a grand time in the little country village. I can still taste the marvelous berries we used to pick in Grandmother's garden—black and red raspberries, currants, and gooseberries too.

Except for the naps she took on the antique couch (we have it still, in our New York apartment), Grandmother Crosby was never idle. Much of the time, she seemed to be cooking; I can remember helping her peel apples, and the smell when she dried them in the oven. Often she sat by the stove in her old rocker, making rag rugs or patchwork quilts. The quilts were never long enough—if you pulled them up under your chin, your toes inevitably emerged from the other end. But they were colorful and gay and fun to make from scraps of old material. I remember how in hot weather my grandparents used to keep cream and butter on a ledge down in the well. Life had a simplicity, a rhythm so pronounced and ordered that it was like hearing the great clock of the universe tick.

If my parents had their worries, or their disagreements (and I'm sure they did), they concealed them from us children. They kept us insulated from pressure—and they didn't force us themselves. They simply let us know that they expected us to do our best, and we responded by trying to outdo each other. It's strange, now, to look back through the years and see how much simpler life was for children in those days. Home was a place where honesty and decency were taught by example, not by decree. School was a place where good behavior was expected, where patriotism was encouraged, where diligence was rewarded. There were no great class or social distinctions—or if there were, I was un-aware of them. Having blithely skipped a couple of grades in grammar school (they let you find your academic level in those unenlightened days without worrying about such things as social maladjustment), I was the youngest girl in my high-school class. My family had neither wealth nor social pretensions. Yet I was president of our homeroom that contained 300 girls, and in my last year vice-president of our Senior Class.

I graduated from Northwestern High School at the age of sixteen and had one year as a freshman at City College in Detroit where tuition was free; all a student had to pay for was books. But then a family dilemma arose. My brother Chuck was at Syracuse University with his senior year com-ing up. Family finances were strained to the utmost. If Chuck was to get his degree—and everyone agreed that he should—some sacrifices would have to be made. At a family conference a decision was reached: I would drop out of college for a year and go to work to help Chuck complete his education. Then, when he had graduated and landed a job, he would repay me by helping me through three more years of college.

I must say, I was not too happy about this solution. I was only seventeen; I was enjoying myself at City College; I knew that all my friends and classmates would move on without me. But I accepted the plan with as much grace as I could muster, and went to work in the commercial department of the M.B.T.C. in Detroit.

I worked there for a little more than a year, and although I wasn't aware of it, the truth my father had tried to teach me about hidden blessings in adversity was working to my advantage all the time. The responsibilities of a job made me mature much faster and showed me, in a dramatically convincing way, the great advantages of a college education.

When I did resume my studies it was with my proper age group and I went to Syracuse University where I could experience all the rewarding activities on a college campus. But the chief benefit was that the delay of a year made it possible for me to meet the man I was destined to spend my life with. If I hadn't spent that year working for the telephone company, I would have graduated and left Syracuse before Norman arrived there.

True to his promise, Chuck sent me money to help me through my three remaining years of college. My first year at Syracuse I lived in a dormitory. The last two I was in a sorority house—Alpha Phi—and earned room and board by acting as manager. Even so, by the time I graduated I owed my brother more than $2,000—no little sum for those days. I paid it back as fast as I could, once I was out of college, with money earned teaching school in Syracuse. I remember that Chuck and I took out life insurance policies on each other's lives—just in case!

I majored in mathematics; I loved the precision and clarity of figures, the sense that my mind was being trained in systematic thinking and logic. And my studies always went well. But there were so many other sides of life to be explored! Dates and dances, football games and roadsters with rumble seats. Just being in a sorority house was an important part of a girl's education. Freshmen had to learn to serve and preside over a formal tea party. Solemn dinners to which faculty members were invited were given once a month. On one occasion we invited the Chancellor's wife. She asked if she might bring her small son, and of course we had to agree. The bored youngster amused himself by flipping pats of butter onto the ceiling whenever his mother wasn't looking. There was nothing in the etiquette manuals that told us how to handle this; by some miracle the suppressed shock and the stifled laughter were not noticed by the Chancellor's wife.

My first college roommate, assigned by chance, was a dark-eyed girl from the St. Lawrence River region. She was somewhat older than I . . . and a lot more experienced in certain areas. I was amazed by what seemed to be her instantaneous popularity: She had a date every night, and apparently could have had a dozen, judging from the way the telephone calls came flooding in to her. It took a more sophisticated classmate to reveal the truth to me: My roommate was a girl who couldn't—and didn't—say No. Before long, the college authorities reached the same conclusion. I tried to defend the black sheep, but had no success. She was told to leave, and she did.

In my junior year, which was my second at Syracuse University, I moved into the sorority house and had four roommates who shared a study-sitting room. One, Phyllis Leonard, was the daughter of a bishop. She and I used to discuss the pros and cons—mostly the cons—of being a minister's daughter. We proclaimed—and our roommates loudly agreed

—that the last thing we'd ever do was marry a minister, with all the self-denial and self-discipline and fishbowl living that such a role required.

In the end, of the five of us, four married ministers, and the fifth chose a man named Mr. Parson!

I heard about Norman for some time before I met him. Girls at the sorority house who went to his church on Sundays came back sighing romantically about the handsome young minister—miraculously unmarried at the age of twenty-nine—who held his congregation spellbound with sermons so eloquent and enthusiastic that going to church became an adventure, not an obligation. He emphasized that religion could be a joyous, exciting, life-giving thing. He had a great sense of humor that appealed particularly to young people; sometimes waves of laughter swept over the congregation in the great nave of the stately University Church. Outside the church he was said to be friendly, sociable and easygoing. But when he stood up in the pulpit there was also an aura of great spiritual authority about him.

"You really ought to meet him, Ruth," my roommate Phyllis Leonard kept saying. "Or at least come to hear him preach. He's from the mid-west, like you—Ohio, I think. I know you'd like him."

"That's just the trouble," I said. "The last thing I want to do is find myself liking an unmarried minister."

I wonder, sometimes, if the spiritual side of our nature, which is timeless, doesn't have the gift of prescience, of knowing what lies ahead. As Emerson says somewhere, "The soul contains the event that shall befall it." It may be fanciful, but I believe that something in me even then was dimly aware that my destiny was linked with this unseen young man that all the girls were talking about. My conscious mind, determined to avoid any entangling alliances with ministers, rejected these signals from the unconscious —rejected them so strongly that I kept thinking up excuses why I *shouldn't* meet this Ohio paragon or go to hear him preach. I was too busy. I had too many dates as it was. I was going to another church that suited me just fine. And so on.

But one night Phyllis persuaded me to go with her to a party being given by the young people's group at the University Church. And, just to stop her from harping on the subject any longer, I went.

It was a gay evening with lots of interesting young people and the time passed very quickly. Phyllis and I were about to leave when she said, "Ruth, you haven't even met Norman Peale. Come on, I will introduce you."

We went across the room and Phyllis said, "Mr. Peale, this is my roommate, Ruth Stafford."

We shook hands. And then a surprising thing happened. He held my hand just a fraction of a second longer than was necessary! I thought to myself, "*This* is going to be interesting!"

And it was. He was a bit embarrassed at calling a young college girl, but he telephoned quite frequently. He said there were committees on which he wanted me to serve, especially one planning a big banquet for all the college young people, with Ralph Sockman from New York as the speaker. Would I be chairman of the committee?

Planning for this affair, I remember one evening when he asked me to help him arrange the seating at the head table. We worked for quite a while and finally had everyone placed except for two empty seats together. "Who are these for?" I wanted to know. "Well," said Norman, "isn't it amazing? They must be for us!" And so they were.

One day he finally asked me out for dinner—following the Sunday morning church service. After accepting, I discovered he was to make a commencement speech that afternoon in a town about twenty-five miles away. Did I mind? We could have dinner on the way. I ended up driving the car, so he could concentrate on the last-minute thoughts for his commencement address!

More and more I became aware that he was using me as a sounding board—testing ideas, trying out possible themes for sermons, seeking my reaction. He could be quite self-centered about this at times. I remember one trip to Cazenovia where he was to give a talk that he called "Imprisoned Splendor," all about the shining potentials locked up inside all of us. He told me about it on the way to Cazenovia. He told me again as we had lunch at the old Linklaen House. He gave his talk and it went very well. Then, on the way home, he again suggested I drive. And while I battled the Sunday traffic he told me all about "Imprisoned Splendor" for the fourth time!

But I didn't mind. When I saw how stirred his audiences were, how people went away from hearing him uplifted and encouraged, I felt that it would be a privilege to be a part—any part—of the creative process that made such eloquence and effectiveness possible.

As our friendship deepened, though, I began to realize that Norman's eloquence and creativity carried a price tag, and that price tag was a constant vulnerability to self-doubt, a hypersensitivity to any negative consideration where his work was concerned. Once in the early days of our courtship he asked me to tell him frankly what I thought of one of his sermons. So I told him frankly that in my opinion, while the beginning was effective, it sagged off a bit at the end. His reaction was one of complete despair. Overwhelmed with gloom, he told me that I had confirmed what he had long suspected: that he'd never be an effective preacher. He was clearly in the wrong profession. Perhaps he should get out of the ministry before it was too late.

Startled and dismayed, I struggled to correct my blunder . . . and finally succeeded. But I had learned a lesson that I have had to live with ever since, namely, that the highly creative person does not want objective criticism even when he thinks he does, or when he asks for it. He wants reassurance. He needs help and support in the endless, exhausting battle that he fights with his own merciless perfectionism. Therefore the approach should never be: "That's all wrong," or, "You did that badly." The approach should be: "This is a great paragraph (or sentence, or idea, or approach) that you've got here. Now, what would you think of trying it like this?"

I know that it all sounds a bit laughable, and Norman and I have laughed over it many times. But if, as a somewhat naive college co-ed, I had failed to learn that lesson quickly and completely and finally, I doubt if we ever would have been married.

Another thing I had to learn (and I truly think God gave me the wisdom, because in those days I had little of my own) was that whatever Norman's basic characteristics were, they were not going to change. He was a grown man, twenty-nine years old, with his character fully formed, all its great gifts and talents and potentials established, but all its defects, too. If I was going to love him (and I was falling as deeply and rapidly in love as a girl ever did), if I was going to share his life and bear his children and help him reach out and transform lives, I was going to have to take him as he was and adapt my own personality to his.

And there was only one way to do this: study the man. Learn everything about him. Learn to know him better than he knew himself. Learn to analyze his needs as coolly as if they were problems in mathematics that needed solutions. Learn what sort of fuel his personality required for maximum performance, find the right mixture, and supply it.

I think I sensed even then, as a girl just out of my teens, that this would be a challenging and formidable task, one that would require all the balance and brains and self-control that I could possibly summon to my aid. What I did not know then, what I do know now, is that when the challenge is met and mastered, nothing in the world is so exciting and satisfying and rewarding.

Our romance progressed swiftly as the days lengthened and the trees showed feathers of green. Too swiftly, I think, for Norman's mother. She came at his invitation to preach the Mother's Day sermon in the University Church. I was impressed. It was clear that much of Norman's gift with words, much of his imagination, much of the romantic element in his makeup came from her.

Unfortunately, Mother Peale was not equally impressed with me. She had great plans, great dreams for Norman. She had accepted the restrictions of life as a small-town minister's wife herself, but she believed her oldest boy had the seeds of greatness in him. She was not unconscious of the value of wealth and social position—and when she looked at me, she could see neither in my family background. She was friendly and polite, but also a bit distant. After all, her son was on the threshold of a brilliant career, already listed in *Who's Who in America,* clearly marked for high honors some day. The Syracuse newspaper had referred to him as the most eligible bachelor in town. That meant that he could have almost any girl for the asking. There was, in particular, a certain banker's daughter whose infatuation with him was well known. Why on earth would he overlook a girl like this, a girl who as a wife could open all sorts of doors for him, and turn instead to a little co-ed from Detroit barely out of her teens?

It made no sense to Mother Peale. She didn't directly try to discourage Norman, but she made it clear that if we became engaged she hoped it would be a long engagement. Very long.

It was. After I graduated, Norman helped me find a teaching job. I taught mathematics at Central High School in Syracuse at a salary of $1,800 per year (Norman was making a princely $5,500). Part of my salary went toward paying off my debt to Chuck; Norman was also helping his younger brother with his educational expenses. Now and then he would give a talk or a baccalaureate address and receive an honorarium of $10 or $15. All around us the country seemed to be riding a dizzy wave of prosperity as the "Roaring Twenties" drew to a close. But I had to count my pennies carefully.

I shared an apartment with an older woman. Every evening Norman would come over. Our engagement was not yet announced, and so we had to be rather circumspect about this. At one point, I remember, we even decided it might be a good idea if Norman were seen occasionally with another girl, just to keep tongues from wagging. And as a matter of fact, tongues did wag. One night two spinster ladies on the Syracuse faculty asked Norman to dinner. They thought it their duty, they said, to let him know that people were talking about his preoccupation with that young Stafford girl. Oh, she might be quite a nice girl, but after all, was she really qualified for a man in his position? Surely he could find someone more sophisticated, someone with more background, someone more—well, more impressive than a high school mathematics teacher.

Somewhat shaken by all this, Norman came straight from the spinster ladies and told me everything they had said. It didn't occur to him that this sort of evaluation could be painful, or even infuriating, to me. What he really wanted was for me to tell him that he wasn't making a terrible mistake in allowing himself to fall in love with me! I remember how I kept silent, fighting to control myself. He's been hurt and upset, I told myself, he wants someone to share that hurt, relieve that upset. He's not thinking right now about my feelings; he's too preoccupied with his own.

And you might as well face it, I told myself, there are going to be other occasions like this, other times when vou'll have to swallow your pride and put your own hurt feelings aside and accept this difficult role of soother and supporter. You had better ask yourself two questions right now, and give yourself honest answers. Can you do it? And is it worth it? I think my head answered the first question: Yes, I can do it if I make myself do it. And my heart answered the second: Yes, oh, yes, it is!

Two years after I had graduated from Syracuse, Norman and I were married in the University Church in Syracuse on a blue-and-gold June day. I knew as we walked out of the church together that a great adventure was beginning for both of us.

Now, after all these years, I never cease to marvel at what a rich and rewarding pilgrimage it has been.

❧ 3 ❧

STUDY
YOUR
MAN

❧ If I could give one piece of advice to young brides, and only one, it would be this: *study your man.* Study him as if he were some rare and strange and fascinating animal, which he is. Study him constantly, because he will be constantly changing. Study his likes and dislikes, his strengths and weaknesses, his moods and mannerisms. Just loving a man is fine, but it's not enough. To live with one successfully you have to know him, and to know him you have to study him.

Look around you and decide how many of the best marriages you know are ones where a wife in a deep sense actually knows her husband better than he knows himself. Knows what pleases him. Knows what upsets him. Knows what makes him laugh or makes him angry. Knows when he needs encouragement. Knows when he's too charged up about something and needs to be held back. Knows, in other words, exactly what makes him tick.

On the other hand, the divorce courts are full of women who didn't study their men, who didn't try to anticipate and meet their needs, who failed to observe warning signs while there was still time to do something about them.

Years ago, I remember, we knew a young clergyman whose father was a distinguished bishop. The first time we

27

met him I was mildly surprised to see that, along with his immaculate white shirt and sober dark suit, he was wearing a pair of flaming red socks. This was in the days before men's fashions began to rival the rainbow. The socks intrigued me so that I mentioned them to Norman.

"Yes," said Norman, "they do seem a bit flamboyant, don't they? I understand that some members of his congregation think so too. They aren't happy about those fire-engine socks, and they've told him so, but he wears them anyway."

"Why on earth," I said, "would a quiet, conservative bishop's son do a thing like 'that?"

"Maybe," said Norman, half joking, "it's to prove that he isn't just a quiet, conservative bishop's son."

The young clergyman was married to a very proper and conventional young woman who was very active in the parish doing all sorts of charities and church work. They seemed, on the surface, quite a well-matched pair. Imagine the sensation, then, when one fine day, out of an apparently blue sky, the young minister left town and took with him the organist of the church, a blonde and lively lady whose husband had died a year or so before. He left a note saying that he was sorry for the scandal he was causing, but that he had stood being a minister as long as he could, that he had found at last a woman who understood him, and that he would marry her as soon as his wife saw fit to give him a divorce. Which she ultimately did.

Who knows how many signs and signals of unhappiness and frustration—aside from his flaming socks—that young man displayed through the years before he made his desperate move? No one can condone what he did, but in my opinion his wife was either incredibly selfish or incredibly blind. She must have had hundreds of indications through the years that her husband was miserable in a profession that no doubt had been thrust upon him by his illustrious father. Under such circumstances, her primary job was not to go around doing good deeds in the community. It was to sense her man's distress and seek a remedy for it, even if it meant changing her way of life completely. But she failed to do this, and one day her way of life blew up in her face.

Studying your man never stops. After our long courtship I felt that I knew Norman inside and out and was ready for anything. But nothing could be further from the fact.

I soon discovered that in one respect my husband and I were exactly opposite. I never had any problem making up my mind about almost anything, but he had a hard time making decisions: should he accept this speaking engagement, should he go to this meeting, should we accept or decline this invitation, what emphasis should he make in this speech. When he asked for my advice, the questions always seemed to come at the most inconvenient times in my well-planned day. But I would stop and listen patiently. Most of the time he just needed me as a sounding board to help clarify his thinking. And I would go away silently congratulating myself on my patience and understanding, being very glad that the matter was settled.

Many times, to my astonishment, I found the next day that the matter was not settled at all, that he wanted to review it again, that maybe there were angles we had not considered seriously enough. And after another lengthy listening period I would go away realizing his thinking today was almost opposite to his conclusion of yesterday!

Then there were times when plans had been made and I was well along in carrying them out when suddenly Norman would tell me that something had come up to change it all, that this new opportunity was far more important, that we weren't going to do what I thought after all.

This became a major adjustment for me, a fundamental

clash in personal characteristics. What could I do? What should I do? Being absolutely honest with myself I knew that Norman's way was often best, that I was too rigid, that if God was going to guide our lives we had to keep our minds open. Norman waited decisions out, and his guidance proved accurate in an uncanny number of times.

Well, I have been practicing this for all these years and it is still hard. And I know it always will be. Even today I listened patiently, and I will have to do the same thing tomorrow. Sometimes I think it is such a waste of time; why can't I change him; do I have to make this adjustment forever?

The answer is yes. It is never finished.

However, I can say this; if I have developed any real strength of character in my life it is because I realize that only a woman can be a wife, and only a wife can give this kind of help to her husband. No task is as difficult as this, but the rewards are tremendous.

Norman has had to make plenty of adjustment to me— but that is his story.

Some husbands need a wife who entertains beautifully and easily. Some require a gay, lively, fun-loving wife. Some must have a quiet, well-organized home. Norman is one of these. Our home is his only haven in an incredibly busy life. And it must be in perfect order.

Now to me there are some things more important than having everything always in place. It doesn't bother me if the morning newspaper is still on the coffee table at night. But not Norman! His creativity simply stops if anything is out of order.

I studied my husband. He is a public speaker and writer with all the sensitivity, even tension, that seems to go with those talents. He has a practical approach in both writing and speaking, an orderly sequence of ideas. And I gradually came to realize that order in the home or in his office, indeed in his entire conduct of affairs, was essential to his creativity.

So I taught myself to have my entire house in perfect order at all times. (I never knew which room he would look in next!) And I like to think my husband has done a better job in life because I studied these traits of his. Certainly it has brought us close together.

Every bride should be made to realize, somehow, that the way a man feels about a woman depends ultimately on the way she makes him feel. If he has deep needs, emotional, physical, or psychological that he expects her to satisfy, and she fails to satisfy them, it will be very hard in the long run for him to give her the affection, admiration, and loyalty that she needs and wants from him.

Of course, a woman has her needs too, and her husband has an equal responsibility to satisfy them. But I honestly think that in the majority of the cases of marital discord that Norman and I have observed over the years, it's the woman who is failing to recognize and meet some basic need in the man.

Often it is something as fundamental as sex. We have seen case after case where the husband complains that the wife is too tired, too busy, or too cold to be an adequate sex partner. Almost always, in such cases, the woman misjudges the urgency of the need in her husband. And then she is hurt and astonished when that unfulfilled need impels him to look elsewhere.

Just last week a couple from an upstate town came to ask our help with precisely this problem. They were in their mid-forties, a typical American middle-class couple. Conventional, conservative, soberly dressed, they were the last people you'd expect to find involved in a triangle situation. But they were. The man had been having an affair with a divorcée who lived down the street. The wife, learning about it, had gone to the divorcée's house while her husband was there. There had been a bitter scene with accusations and recriminations. It was clear that the problem was far from resolved. But they wanted us to help them resolve it.

Sometimes these discussions can be brutally frank, and this one was. The woman berated her husband for his lack of loyalty. The husband was not proud of himself, but he was not contrite either. "You," he said, pointing a finger at his wife, "are a dog in the manger. You don't like sex. You never have. But you don't want anyone else to enjoy it!"

"Why don't you act your age?" the wife retorted angrily. "That's all kid stuff, and you know it! People at our stage of life shouldn't have to worry about that kind of nonsense!"

We tried to make the wife see that it wasn't nonsense, that it was precisely this attitude that had driven her husband into the arms of another woman, that if she wanted him back she would have to be more understanding and more cooperative. But it was hard going, because in her mind her own preferences came before her husband's needs.

I remember Norman saying to her, "Look, sex in marriage isn't just a physical act of gratification. It's an expression of love, of loyalty, of affection—all the things that I'm sure you yourself want most. Can't you see that?"

"Perhaps," said the woman grudgingly. "But how long can that sort of thing go on?"

"In your case," said Norman cheerfully, "I'd say for at least another thirty years!"

They smiled at that, and you could feel some of the tension go out of the air. They went away, finally, saying that they would try to forget the past and regain the closeness they once had known. And I think they will because the wife admitted her failing and promised to try to understand her husband's needs.

One of the saddest consequences of failing to study your

mate, I think, is to have him slowly outgrow you. Not long ago a man came to Norman and said that after twenty-five years of marriage he was going to leave his wife. Norman asked the usual questions: Was there deep disagreement that they couldn't resolve? Was there some other woman in the picture?

No, the man said, it was none of these things. There was no quarrel; he wasn't in love with someone else. But he was bored, bored beyond all reason, beyond endurance. "While the children were still at home," he said, "my wife had something to do, some purpose in life. But now that they're gone, she has none. She has absolutely no outside interests. She has no friends. She talks incessantly—about nothing. She knows nothing about what's going on in the world. I just dread going home in the evening. I can't stand it any longer."

"Can't you share some of your interests with her?" Norman asked. "Can't you draw her into some of your own hobbies or interests?"

"It's too late," the man said. "Maybe if we'd started sharing them fifteen years ago we'd have had a chance to-day. But we didn't. We stayed together because we were raising a family, but we were growing at different rates. Now we're two different people, with nothing in common. I'm going to ask her for a divorce." And he did.

The moral is plain enough: Studying your mate should include a willingness to participate, at least occasionally, in activities that interest him (or her) more than they in-terest you. Some domestically-oriented women never learn to do this. Their husbands may be ardent golfers, or gar-deners, or bowlers, or bridge players, but the women they have married make no effort to join them in the areas where they are happiest and where in most cases they would welcome the companionship of a wife. A few men may really prefer to escape from their wives into all-male activities, but very often they have no choice, because their wives won't follow them anyway.

Sometimes a pretended interest can become a real one. I knew a woman once, married to a fanatical trout fisherman, who made herself go fishing with him even though she didn't know a dry fly from a luna moth. At first she was horribly bored, baffled by the intricacies of the sport, sure that she could never acquire even the most rudimentary skill. But gradually her attitude changed. Her husband's enthusiasm was contagious, his delight in teaching her was endearing. In the end, although she never became an expert, she was able to participate with an enthusiasm and enjoyment that at first she would have thought impossible. And it all came about because, studying her husband, trying to make him happy, she enlarged her own horizons.

In a way, this also happened to me. When I was first married, I had no real experience or deep interest in church affairs. I knew nothing of board meetings or committee functions. I certainly could not see myself presiding over one. But it soon became apparent that this was an area where I could be of great use to Norman. Studying him made me realize that this sort of activity was not one of his strong points. Organizational work left him impatient and restless. He was at his best when he was preaching, or writing, or dealing with the emotional difficulties of individuals. I began to see that if I could take some of the organizational work off his back, go to the committee meetings, report back, summarize, simplify, help Norman make the big decisions and spare him from having to make the little ones, I would be making an enormous contribution— one that would make me even more indispensable to him, one that would win for me, on an ever-increasing scale, his affection and gratitude and esteem.

So I did it. I studied the organizational structure of the

church. I learned how to conduct meetings. I practically memorized Robert's Rules of Order. In the process I made a surprising discovery about myself: I was rather good at this sort of thing! People said that I made a good discussion leader, that I had a knack for grasping the essence of a problem, brushing aside irrelevant detail, getting to the point. What began as a slightly apprehensive decision to do something useful for Norman became a whole new dimension in my own life, one that has expanded steadily ever since. When I look back, I am astonished and humbled at the honors in this field that have come my way. My own listing in *Who's Who in America* has nothing to do with being Norman's wife but represents my own career. Thus, when I say that being a wife is the greatest career a woman can have I do it from the vantage point of a career woman.

Having some outside interests of her own will often keep a wife from feeling jealous of her husband's achievements. But she has to keep a wary eye on his masculine ego, which can easily be bruised or damaged. Not long ago I read a magazine article in which a marriage counselor described a situation where a husband became moody and irascible when his wife took a job. "In this case," the marriage counselor explained, "although the husband agreed intellectually with the wife's decision to go to work, he couldn't accept it emotionally. Having a working wife made him feel inadequate as the family provider, so he became defensive and over-sensitive to every real or imagined threat to his masculinity."

I don't mean to imply in any way that it is not perfectly proper for a wife to work. But she will find it very important to study her man's reactions, and not do anything that will lower his self-esteem and in turn damage their marriage.

The wife who studies her husband over the years—really studies him—will come to know him even better than he knows himself. She will be aware of qualities and potentialities in him that he himself may not know are there.

I thought of this the other day when I heard a story about a certain wife in a small midwestern town, a gentle, sweet-tempered woman whose husband was a gay blade, very attractive to women. He knew it, and he took advantage of it at every opportunity—and there were lots of opportunities.

Since it was a small town, this man's amorous adventures were a matter of common knowledge. And since it was a typical small town, there were those who considered it their duty—their somewhat gleeful duty—to tell the wife about the husband's philanderings.

But the curious thing was that these bearers of ill-tidings never seemed to get anywhere with the wife. She would listen patiently to the worst they had to say, then she would smile and reply that she was quite sure they were mistaken. Her Bob was not that kind of man at all. He would be incapable of such deceit. She appreciated their interest, but they really need not concern themselves further, because obviously they didn't know what they were talking about.

The informers kept trying. But against this serene assurance, against this unshakable faith (for that is what it seemed to be) they made no headway whatever.

Meantime, because nothing remains secret in small towns, reports of his wife's attitude got back to the husband. At first he congratulated himself on having a wife whose suspicions were so hard to arouse. He told himself that it made his extra-marital exploits a lot less risky. In fact, it just went to prove his long-time contention that what a wife didn't know wouldn't hurt her.

But gradually a change came over this man. He stopped looking for adventures, and he ceased being responsive when adventurers came looking for him. The townspeople were amazed. One day a man who knew him well asked him what had come over him.

"Well," he said, "I think I could have stood up to any sort of complaint or recrimination from Martha, any wifely jealousy, any amount of anger or accusation. But the one thing I couldn't do was brush off her faith in me. If she thought I was a hero, how could I go on being such a heel? I tried to go on, actually, but I found I just couldn't. I owe her a lot. I'm going to spend the rest of my life trying to make it up to her."

Was that wife simply naive, innocent, starry-eyed? Or did she know her husband better than he knew himself?

Who can say?

⚜ 4 ⚜

FUN IS WHERE
YOU
MAKE IT

⚜ It's astonishing, in this age of wonders, how often people—even young people—come up to me and complain that they're bored. Life is so monotonous, they say. It's dull. It has lost its flavor. Nothing is much fun any more.

Now I know that a share of unhappiness comes to everyone in this life, and it's true that some people have valid cause to be downhearted. But when the average person complains that he's bored, nine times out of ten it's because he isn't making much effort to be anything else. He isn't putting any fun into life, and that's why he isn't getting any out.

It seems to me that all important areas of life should be flavored with fun—marriage, job, housework, friendships, even religion. I've always liked the story of the little boy on his first trip to New York whose parents brought him to a Sunday service at Marble Collegiate Church. The family sat in the gallery where they had a fine view of everything. Norman was in rare form that morning, and his sermon was full of stories taken from everyday life, some of which had their humorous side. The little boy looked down in wonderment at all the happy faces, then turned to his parents. "This can't be a church," he whispered, "everybody's having *fun!*"

Well, why not? Laughter is one of God's most special gifts to man. "Rejoice!" the Bible says over and over. And "a merry heart doeth good like a medicine." One Thanksgiving years ago Norman preached on this topic. The very next Sunday one lively young couple responded to his exhortation to let religion be fun by putting a well-dried turkey wishbone in the collection plate!

One of the chief ingredients of fun is a sense of humor, and most good senses of humor include a sense of the ridiculous. Norman and I still laugh over an episode that happened early in our marriage. Norman was the young minister in charge of the staid and impressive University Church in Syracuse. Somewhat in awe of the dignified deans and erudite professors who were in his congregation, he took pains never to say or do anything unconventional or bizarre. He was always very proper indeed.

One summer afternoon, coming home from the church, he passed by the house of an elderly spinster named Miss Foote, who was also a member of his congregation. Miss Foote was in her front yard looking distractedly for her favorite cat, which apparently had run away.

Norman says that I was forever lecturing him on the importance of always helping his parishioners, no matter what their problem might be. So he offered to help Miss Foote find her cat. "Where did you see him last?" Norman wanted to know. "Right over there," cried Miss Foote. "I think he went through that hole in the hedge!"

The hole was a small one, but Norman gallantly got down on his hands and knees and started crawling through it. Twigs and leaves rained down upon him, brambles pulled his glasses askew, but he kept going until suddenly his head emerged on the far side of the hedge about eighteen inches above a sidewalk. There was no sign of the cat, but on the sidewalk was a pair of feet belonging to a pedestrian who had halted in amazement. Looking up, Norman saw the austere countenance of Professor Perley O. Place, the most imperious and forbidding member of the entire faculty. The gaze of incredulity and disapproval that the professor bestowed upon his spiritual guide and counselor was so paralyzing that Norman couldn't even attempt an explanation. All he could say was, "Good evening, Professor!"

"Extraordinary!" murmured the learned pedagogue frostily. "Most extraordinary!" And he stalked away.

One way to have fun in your life is to associate with "fun" people. Some people carry an indefinable air of gaiety around with them, and they're well worth cultivating, because often that gaiety will rub off on you. We have a friend like that named Millard Bennett. Millard is a jovial soul who often gives lectures at business conventions on the psychology of selling. For a while he and Norman went around giving talks together. Norman always insisted on speaking first, because he claimed that Millard was so good that any speaker who followed him was bound to be an anticlimax.

Millard's favorite topic was persuasion. Anyone, he used to say, could persuade anyone else to walk the road of agreement if only he would use the right approach. "A man," he would tell his audience, "can talk to his wife in two ways. He can say, 'Dear, your face would stop a clock,' and she would be humiliated and hurt. Or he can say, lovingly, 'Darling, when I look at you, time stands still.'" The idea was the same, Millard said, but the way it was phrased made quite a difference!

Millard had one story that went on for at least fifteen minutes about how he persuaded his wife one night, under the most adverse circumstances, to fetch him a glass of water. As he told it, the unsuspecting wife was sorting out some beads on the divan where she was sitting. She had them all classified as to size and color, and the last thing she wanted to do was disturb them, as she would have to do if she stood up. But, ever the psychologist, Millard set himself the problem of persuading her to bring him a glass of water, which he really didn't want at all.

First he told her how pleasant it was to be alone with her on a winter evening with the fire crackling on the hearth. Next he observed that marrying her was probably the smartest move of his life. Then he began to praise her homemaking ability; no one, he assured her, could cook the way she did.

All this time he had been thumbing through a magazine. "Now, here's an advertisement about a ham," he said. "It looks pretty good, but it couldn't hold a candle to the ones you bake." He sighed plaintively. "By the way, is that ham you cooked yesterday still in the kitchen? A ham sandwich certainly would taste good right now."

Up jumped the proud and happy wife, scattering her beads in all directions, and went into the kitchen to fix the sandwich. Whereupon Millard called out that he had changed his mind. "Don't bother about the sandwich, dear," he said. "But while you're up, would you just bring me a glass of water?"

My telling of the story doesn't do justice to it, but Millard always had his audience in stitches. He was a fun speaker, and a fun man.

I've been lucky to be married to a very "fun" man. Norman's sense of the dramatic, his interest in everything, and above all his imagination make him a marvelous companion for people of all ages. When our children were small, for example, Norman spent hours telling them stories that he made up on the spur of the moment, right out of his head. This generally took place at the dinner table and the children could hardly wait. I remember one whole series that went on for months about three imaginary characters named Larry, Harry, and Parry. These remarkable young people had a magic airplane that they kept in their pocket until they needed it. If they wanted to go anyplace they would take the airplane, blow on it and, like magic, it became large enough for them to climb aboard and take off. They would soar away to investigate a big, billowy cloud, or to fight with giants, or to live in the forest in the treetops, or to rescue princesses in distant lands. The magic airplane was a very real and exciting phenomenon to our children.

There was another series of stories about a faintly sinister individual named Jake the Snake, who had an even more malevolent brother known as Hake the Snake. The children would listen, spellbound, to the dreadful deeds of the Snake brothers—and to tell the truth, so would I.

Not everyone, to be sure, has the kind of inventiveness and creativity that can lead so effortlessly to spontaneous fun. But I'm convinced that anyone who will work at it can increase his fun capacity. It doesn't require time or money so much as imagination and the willingness to try something new. Any mother can make a meal more interesting by attempting some exotic or unusual dish. Any father, faced with a Sunday afternoon with the children, can think up something interesting or appealing if he'll just put his mind to it. I heard of one busy father who keeps what he calls a "why not?" notebook on his desk at the office. In it he jots down all sorts of offbeat ideas that occur to him during the week: Why not take the children to that fortune teller on the edge of town and get their palms read? Why not go to a pawnshop with them and pawn something? Why not visit a farm and try to milk a cow? He says he has only one criterion for such ideas: They have to be fun—or hold the promise of fun.

One winter in New York I took our children on a once-a-week sightseeing or investigating tour—those things you always put off doing. Among other things we went to the New York City bus terminal, the largest in the world with the fastest escalator. We went to the Statue of Liberty and to the Empire State Building. And there were lots of out-of-the-way places. We had a great time.

Sometimes youngsters can get a bit carried away by the spirit of fun. I remember vividly one summer afternoon when our Margaret and John were about ten and eight respectively. I was having a rather serious meeting of churchwomen in our apartment on Fifth Avenue. Suddenly the doorbell buzzed, and there was one of the doormen of the building looking grave. "Mrs. Peale," he said, "there's a policeman downstairs. He has a complaint. Some one is dropping bombs from your apartment windows into the street."

"Bombs?" I echoed incredulously.

"Water bombs," said the doorman. "Paper bags filled with water—and enough sand to make them fall on people's heads."

"People's *heads?*" In the sudden hush behind me I could sense all my churchwomen listening intently.

"Well," said the doorman, "the bombs missed this lady. But it was a near miss. And her clothes are all splashed, and she is very angry, and she complained to the policeman. And he is downstairs right now . . ."

"You mean," I cried, "that my children are dropping these —these things on passersby? How do you know our children are the culprits?" Behind me I could almost *feel* the craning of necks and the raised eyebrows.

"Because, Mrs. Peale," the doorman said resignedly, "your children have been practicing their—er—bombing techniques in the air shaft on the inside of the building. The bottom of the shaft is full of water and sand and paper bags. I'm afraid Margaret and John are the guilty ones. There's no doubt about it."

Well, I had to summon the guilty ones, send them in disgrace to their rooms, go downstairs, placate the policeman, apologize to the irate lady, arrange to pay for having her clothes cleaned, and assure the doorman that such an aerial assault would never happen again.

I had to tell Norman, of course. We spoke to the children sternly, telling them that their prank might have hurt someone or caused a lawsuit. We made them go down to the bottom of the air shaft and clean up the debris. We made them pay out of their allowance for the irate lady's cleaning bill. I forget, now, what other penalties we imposed. But I must confess, one reaction that both Norman and I had, carefully concealed behind our stern parental exteriors, was a feeling of relief and gratitude that our youngsters did have a sense of fun, even if a bit misguided, that they weren't meek and mild goody-goodies, that they were a pair of high-spirited, fun-loving youngsters, even if they were "preacher's kids."

In too many American homes, I think, parents offer all kinds of excuses and rationalization for the inertia that is the deadly enemy of fun: They can't be bothered to change the routine, they can't afford to, they can't find the time, it's easier to turn on the television set . . . and so on.

But all it takes is a tiny spark of originality. For example, one young couple we know, living on a very tight budget, manage to put aside three or four dollars a week for what they call their mini-honeymoon fund. When it reaches a certain level, they park their children with friends or relatives, take an inexpensive motel room on the edge of town, dress up a bit, have a carefree dinner, and spend the night together away from all the routine and familiarity of daily living. The wife says that these "mini-honeymoons," which happen three or four times a year, give her such a lift that she wouldn't exchange them for anything.

There are endless ways to break up a pattern of living

that has become monotonous. Ask someone you don't know very well to lunch or dinner. Strike up a conversation with a stranger on a bus or a train or a plane (he may learn something; you certainly will). Try your hand at bowling. Or at wallpapering a room. Fly a kite with a small child. Work as a hospital volunteer. Go and sign up for a course in some subject that has always interested you. Try anything that's new or different.

Of course, breaking out of the prison of routine takes some effort. But there's a wonderful world outside. And sawing through the bars is half the fun and another adventure in being a you-can't-tell-what-will-come-next wife.

5

A LOVE
AFFAIR
WITH LIFE

As a rule I don't watch television very often; I seldom seem to find the time. But one evening, quite late, I turned on the set. Artur Rubinstein, the great musician, was being interviewed by some reporter. And he said a wonderful thing.

The reporter was asking questions about Rubinstein's career. How did he account for his success? Was it talent? Was it discipline? Was it hard work? Was it luck? "I don't know," Rubinstein said with a smile. "All I know is that if you love life, life will love you back!"

I've thought of that statement many times since, and often in connection with my husband, Norman. I've never known anyone who loves life in all its aspects more than he does. He loves people—all sorts of people. He loves places— the rich Ohio farmland where he was born, the gentle Berkshire hills where our country home is, the soaring majesty of the Swiss Alps. He loves laughter. He loves his church. He loves the busy life he leads speaking to conventions and community meetings of all kinds all over the world. He loves new ideas, new challenges, new problems to solve.

And, just as Rubinstein said, life seems to love Norman right back. Oh, he has had his share of criticism, and his ups and downs. But life has poured out endless blessings

on him down through the years. His health and energy are
fantastic. He was never in a hospital in his life until a gall
bladder operation became necessary some time ago—and
he bounced back from that so fast that it was amazing. In
no time at all, it seemed, he was back preaching two sermons
every Sunday, writing newspaper columns, taping radio
programs, running the interfaith magazine *Guideposts*,
raising funds for all sorts of worthy causes, acting as President of the Reformed Churches of America, crisscrossing
the country constantly to give talks to conventions and
civic groups—and somehow finding time to listen to the intimate problems of troubled people everywhere.

Where does this energy and creativity come from? I know
what Norman would say. He would say that he tries to keep
as close as possible to the Source of all energy, and live in
such a way that the channels through which that energy
comes are always open. He believes that anyone can live
that way, and receive that energy. This is what he has
always preached: That Christianity is not just a musty set
of beliefs. That it's not a collection of sterile rules. That it
is a storehouse of endless joy and energy, and that the key
that unlocks the storehouse is faith. Norman believes completely that anyone who will use the key can have the kind
of love affair with life that Rubinstein was talking about.
And in many ways it seems to me that his own life is proof
of it.

Because I have been privileged to be a part of his life,
my own has been enriched beyond belief. I have been to
places so glamorous and met people so fascinating that
sometimes I feel like pinching myself to make sure that it's
not a dream—the kind of dream that the little girl behind
the ribbon counter back in Detroit would have been incapable of even imagining.

Let me try to describe one of these encounters just the
way it happened a few months ago. I'll tell about it in the

present tense in an effort to bring it all back clearly, just the way it was. Perhaps you'll see what I mean.

It is July, 1969. Norman and I are flying around the world. President Nixon has asked Norman to go to Viet Nam and give some talks to our soldiers there. I am not going into the war zone with him; while he's there I will wait for him in Thailand (where there are marvelous shops!). On the way out to the Far East we plan a stopover on the island of Formosa, or Taiwan as it's called. The government of Nationalist China knows about our visit and an invitation comes from President Chiang Kai-shek: He and his wife would be pleased to have us visit them at the summer Presidential Residence high up in the mountains in the interior of the island.

Norman and I have long known the Generalissimo and Madame Chiang as old friends. A strong and dedicated Christian, the Generalissimo and his equally spiritual wife have been deeply impressed by some of Norman's writings. On one of our previous trips to Taiwan, Norman has preached in the President's private chapel in Taipei. The Chinese interpreter on that occasion was marvelously quick and intelligent. He introduced Norman as one of the world's great Christians, and Norman jokingly replied, "You're the best interpreter I ever had; please tell the President that." The man said something in Chinese, and everyone laughed. "What did you say?" asked Norman. "I told His Excellency," replied the interpreter, poker-faced, "that you said I was the *worst* interpreter you ever had!"

No matter what country you're in, a visit to a Head of State is surrounded by a great deal of ceremony and protocol, which makes the occasion even more exciting and impressive. We arrive in Taiwan in hot, humid weather. Madame Chiang's personal secretary meets us at the airport and escorts us to the Grand Hotel in Taipei. She explains that on the following day we will take a three-hour train ride, followed by an automobile trip of 150 miles through rugged mountain country. She says that the President and Madame Chiang have arranged a dinner in our honor, and are looking forward to our visit.

The next morning we are driven to the railroad station where the stationmaster has set aside a private room for our convenience. Here, during the short wait, we are served tea and treated with great deference and courtesy. On the train, which is beautifully air-conditioned, four seats have been reserved for us and our escort. An attendant comes through the train offering each passenger complimentary hot towels, rolled up and steaming, with which to wipe your face and hands—very refreshing. The train pulls out, smooth as silk, exactly on time. On the window side of our seats are two wooden holders, each containing a glass. At intervals throughout the trip, a little girl appears carrying a tray with six different kinds of tea bags, followed by a boy with a kettle of boiling water to pour over the tea of your choice. At about noon, we eat a cold lunch from paper boxes; fruit and delicious sandwiches and cold roast pigeon.

Exactly three hours out of Taipei, the train stops. This time we are met by two cars. Why two? Because we might feel a trifle crowded in one! Now begins one of the most spectacular drives I have ever taken anywhere. We follow the Cross-Island highway as it climbs steadily into the mountains. All around us are green cultivated fields and small, neat villages. We have been told that, next to Japan, Taiwan is the most progressive and prosperous country in the Far East. Driving along the superbly engineered highway, it is easy to believe this. Higher and higher we go, along stupendous precipices and gorges, across marble bridges cut literally from mountains of marble, past cloud-capped peaks almost two miles high. The air, no longer hot and muggy, is cool and bracing.

We come at last to the Summer Residence, imposing with

its curved tile roofs and porticos gleaming with red lacquer. We are shown to an elegant suite. Again the inevitable and ceremonial tea is served. We are informed that we will not see our hosts until dinner time, but then we will see them an hour ahead of the other dinner guests. In the meantime, a car is waiting to take us on a sight-seeing drive if we care to go. The President, we're told, would like us to see some of the experimental agricultural projects in the vicinity.

After the drive, we are told to be ready to meet our hosts at seven o'clock. We change into more formal clothes, a dark suit for Norman, a short "dressy" dress for me. Precisely at seven o'clock we are ushered to a handsome living room. A uniformed guard stands at the door. We are alone for three or four minutes, then Madame Chiang comes in looking extraordinarily young and beautiful in a blue Chinese gown. We sit and talk for a while, then an aide announces the President. We all stand. The Generalissimo comes in, a slender figure of great dignity wearing a light-colored uniform. Although he speaks no English, his presence dominates the room. He greets Norman with a warm handshake. Madame Chiang interprets for him. "The President says . . ." "The President would like to know . . ."

After a while, other guests begin to arrive. There are perhaps twenty in all, including a Catholic bishop. The President greets them all, then leaves the room. The rest of us go down to a richly-decorated dining room where a long table is waiting. Place cards tell us where to sit. I am on the right of an empty chair, larger and more ornate than the rest. We all sit briefly. Then a gong sounds and a deep-voiced aide cries in English: "The President of the Republic of China!" Chiang Kai-shek enters and takes his place in the large chair. Norman says grace. The meal begins.

No wine or liquor is served, and the food is delicious. Course after course is served by servants so deft and quick that the plates seem to appear and disappear like magic.

Norman and I bravely use chopsticks and do so well that
Madame Chiang compliments us. Toward the end of the
meal, each of us is served a cup of a delicately flavored
beverage called almond milk, made from crushed almonds.
The President—his wife interpreting—tells us with a smile
about the American government official who, when told
that he was drinking almond milk, cried, "You get this by
feeding almonds to your cows? What a splendid idea!"

After dinner we all go to another magnificent room where
we are shown a movie, a love story set in old China. Soon
after that the other guests depart, and once more we are
alone with our hosts. "Mr. President," Norman says, "you
amaze me. Despite your age you still have a clear eye,
great vigor, unwrinkled skin, perfect health. You just don't
seem to grow old. How do you do it?"

The Generalissimo smiles. "It's simple," he tells us. "I
pray three times a day!"

Madame Chiang translates this for us. Then she adds,
"He says he prays three times a day. What he means is
that he devotes himself to prayer and meditation for thirty
minutes three times a day. No one is allowed to interrupt
or disturb him during these periods for any reason whatsoever."

"Ninety minutes a day in prayer," Norman murmurs.
"How many of us at home have that kind of faith?"

Back in our suite, as we prepare for bed, we find ourselves talking about this remarkable couple. "He's a great
man," Norman says. "You don't trifle with him. And she's
a great—a really great—person in her own right. They've
gone through fire together, those two. Now they're bound
together by the things that really count: mutual respect,
tremendous courage, deep faith."

I nod, thinking of the hostile, left-wing-inspired stories
that have circulated about these two people in the United
States. That the Generalissimo is a ruthless dictator—this

man whose faith in Christian principles is so strong that he once translated the Bible into Mandarin. That his wife is so pampered that wherever she goes she demands silk sheets—when actually she suffers from a skin allergy that makes it necessary for her when traveling to carry along her own special sheets.

But this sort of character assassination, I've observed, is something that seems to happen to people who are outspokenly anti-communist.

Early the next morning, just at dawn, Norman wakes up. It is about five A.M., a cold, clear morning. He gets up, goes to a window, looks out. A moment later he says, "Ruth, are you awake? If you are, come over here for a minute."

Half asleep and shivering, I slip on a dressing gown and join him at the window. On a balcony not fifty yards away, fully dressed and wearing a long robe and a cap, is a slender familiar figure. Followed by a big dog, Chiang Kai-shek is pacing slowly back and forth, head bowed, hands clasped behind him. In the breathless hush of the new day, he stops now and then and looks out over the mountains. Neither Norman nor I say a word. But when we turn away from the window we know we have been watching the President of the Republic of China at prayer.

Later we are served an elaborate breakfast in our suite. Soon after that, Madame Chiang comes to our rooms for a spiritual talk with us. She asks if we would like to listen to a prayer which she adapted from one by the Bishop of Bloemfontein, South Africa. We shall never forget how, in her beautifully modulated, deeply earnest voice she prayed as follows; and she prefaced the prayer by saying it should be said slowly or brooded over; or thought or felt:

A PRAYER FOR QUIET TIME

O Holy Spirit of God,
Come into my heart and fill me;

I open the windows of my soul to let Thee in.
I surrender my whole life to Thee;
Come and possess me, fill me with light and truth.
I offer to Thee the one thing I really possess,
My capacity for being filled by Thee.
Of myself I am an empty vessel.
Fill me so that I may live the life of the Spirit,
The life of Truth and Goodness,
The life of Beauty and Love.
The life of Wisdom and Strength.
And guide me to-day in all things:
Guide me to the people I should meet or help;
To the circumstances in which I can best serve Thee;
Whether by my actions or my sufferings.
But, above all, make Christ to be formed in me,
That I may dethrone self in my heart and make Him
   King;
So that He is in me, and I in Him,
Today and forever.   Amen.

Finally, leaving his affairs of state, Chiang Kai-shek joins us. We talk for a while, then we all join hands and each of us prays—the Generalissimo in Chinese. It is a moment of deep Christian fellowship, tender, affectionate, beautiful.

All too soon, it is time to go. A photographer appears and takes pictures that will be sent to us as mementoes of our visit. We thank our hosts and say good-bye. They stand there close together, smiling and waving as our car pulls away.

Some of the details of our stay on the lovely island of Taiwan have faded, and others no doubt will. But neither of us will ever forget that lonely, majestic figure on the balcony, gazing out over the eternal hills, drawing strength and solace from the power of prayer.

✹ 6 ✹

WHO'S THE
OPTIMIST
IN YOUR HOUSE?

✹ It was one of those isn't-it-a-small-world coin-
cidences. I was on my way to Chicago to join Norman,
who had a speaking engagement there. The woman who
happened to sit beside me in the airplane was a stranger.
But when we identified ourselves, it turned out that during
her visit to New York she had attended a service at the
Marble Church and had heard Norman preach.

"Oh," she cried, "it was such a practical sermon. I came
to church feeling dispirited and depressed, and I went away
feeling like a new woman. I just wish my husband could
have heard that sermon. He certainly could use a lift."

"What's the problem?" I asked her. "What's bothering
your husband?"

She shook her head resignedly. "Everything bothers him!
The state of the world bothers him. The state of his health
bothers him. His job and his finances bother him. He's the
most downbeat, pessimistic man I know. Life in our house
with my husband around is one long gloom."

"Well," I said, "can't you change that?"

"Me?" She looked astonished. "Why, I'm just his wife.
What can I do about it?"

"Everything," I said.

"Oh, come now, Mrs. Peale," she said, half disbelieving

and half indignant. "It's easy for you to talk. You're married to one of the world's great optimists. You haven't any idea of what I'm up against."

"Oh yes, I have," I answered quickly. "Every wife runs into this problem from time to time and I'm no exception. It's true that my husband is a great optimist. He believes in the goodness of life, and the goodness in people. But he has his moments of discouragement, too. And believe me, his outlook can turn quite dark. When he gets depressed, he sees only the negative side of everything. Sometimes I think he writes about positive thinking because he understands so much about negative thinking! Of course, he knows that it doesn't get him anywhere, and he can and does come out of these moods. But I consider it part of my job as a wife to understand all this, to evaluate it unemotionally, and then do something about it."

"Do something about it?" she said with surprise. "Why, all I want to do is get out of the house and leave my husband alone with his miserable thoughts and hope he will come out of it quickly."

"Oh, no," I responded in dismay. "You're taking the easy way out, and in the process you're missing a chance to make your job as a wife into an adventure."

"Well, I never heard anything like that, Mrs. Peale," my newfound friend replied. "How do you do it? I mean, how do you help your husband when he is depressed? You almost make it sound as if my husband's pessimism were my fault!"

"Maybe to some extent it is," I said. "I think the wife is the one who can set the emotional climate of the home. Basically, women are more stable emotionally than men— although most men won't admit it. Women are not so vulnerable to disappointment. They're used to soothing hurt feelings and bandaging skinned knees. Ten thousand years ago, when the hunters came back to the cave day after day empty-handed, and the sabre-toothed tiger howled outside, who do you think said, 'Don't worry; everything will be all right'? Was it the brawny caveman? It was not! It was the cavewoman, and she's been saying it ever since."

"That may be true," my companion said stubbornly. "But I still don't think you realize how contagious pessimism can be."

"No more contagious than optimism," I said. "But let's take this problem and go at it logically for a few minutes. To begin with, is there anything really seriously wrong with your husband's health or his finances?"

"No," she said. "It's all a state of mind."

"All right," I said, "let's consider your tactics. When your husband starts complaining or grumbling or finding fault with things, what's your reaction? Do you really leave the house, or what exactly do you do?"

"Usually I urge him not to be such a complainer. I tell him he's getting me down. I invite him to shut up."

"That's understandable." I said, "but is it wise? Isn't it possible that by shutting him up you're just bottling up all his fears or worries inside of him? Mightn't it be smarter to encourage him to talk, to verbalize all his frustrations, get them out of his system? Maybe one reason he's full of gloom is that he can never really get rid of it, never truly unburden himself. Maybe you need to learn to absorb some of it for him, as if you were made of emotional blotting paper. That's what I do when my husband gets discouraged. I urge him to talk it out. Believe me, it shortens the period of depression enormously."

"Well," she said, "that makes a lot of sense. But he gets me so upset. I answer him back and before you know it I'm mad and he's mad and it's terrible."

"That isn't being 'emotional blotting paper.' You really have to learn to absorb what is on his mind as he talks it out. Maybe you need some techniques in order to do this."

"Like what?" she asked.

"Oh, there are many. For instance, listen, but don't listen —let it go in one ear and out the other and above all, don't react emotionally to it. Or count to ten. Or look at your husband and think how much you love him. Don't say that aloud. It isn't the right moment. Just think it. And keep thinking of yourself as blotting paper."

"That sure is a new idea," she said thoughtfully. "Do you really do it?"

"Yes," I said, "and you can too."

"Is there anything else?" She had fully convinced me that she wanted help.

"Since you ask," I said with a smile, "I'll suggest a few other things. First, stop thinking of yourself as 'only a wife.' You can influence your husband more than any other person in the world. Make up your mind that you're going to help him with this problem, instead of just enduring it.

"Now what, specifically, can a woman with a gloomy husband do? She can try to change his state of mind by changing what goes into his mind. If he were suffering from a vitamin deficiency, you'd change his diet, wouldn't you? Well, you can change his mental diet, too.

"I've noticed that people who are depressed or gloomy seem to enjoy reading or hearing gloomy things. Try to counteract this tendency. If you take the gloom-peddlers at face value nowadays you'd think that the country has failed, society has failed, the church has failed, everything is going to the dogs. But that's just not so. Point out to your husband that it isn't so. Do a lot of upbeat reading yourself so you always have a story to tell that counteracts this kind of news-distortion.

"Next, look for every exciting, hopeful, optimistic item you can find in your daily life and pass it on to your husband. If a preacher says something that gives you a lift, hurry home and tell him what it was. Better still, next Sunday ask him to go with you to hear that preacher! If you come across a story that reflects the innate courage or kindness or determination in people, make sure that your husband knows about it too. Feed upbeat things into your conversation with him. Deep down, he must be hungry for this sort of encouragement. In fact, he must be starved for it!"

"I'm sure he is, poor man," she murmured.

"Most people are," I told her. "Twenty-five years ago my husband and I and a friend of ours named Raymond Thornburg started a magazine called *Guideposts*. It has had tremendous success precisely because it fills every issue with true stories of this kind, stories of people who overcome obstacles, who find strength and joy in helping others, who have learned to live positively and happily, who don't let handicaps hold them back or get them down. It's exciting and inspirational and really upbeat all the way. It helps millions of people. It might help your husband too."

"Tell me how I can get it," she said.* "And there's another thing I'm going to do, too. I'm going to try to steer my husband away from people who are downbeat and pessimistic and negative. I'm going to invite positive, clear-thinking people to our home. I can see now that my husband's attitude has attracted a whole lot of pessimists and I'm going to steer him away from them. I can do it and I will!"

"There are a couple of simple exercises," I said, "that you might try—or persuade your husband to try. Just for fun, take a paper and pencil and write down all the good things you can think of about your life together. Or the place where you live. Or a friend that you both know and like. The human mind can't hold two sets of ideas simultaneously. If you make yourself focus on something good, you can't at the same time dwell on something bad.

* Write *Guideposts* Magazine, Carmel, New York 10512.

"And here's another discipline. For one whole day, try to avoid saying anything critical or derogatory about anybody. You may think something negative about somebody, but don't put it into words. This is harder to do than you might suppose. But if you slip on Monday, try again on Tuesday. Keep trying until you've done it for a whole day. Then do it again. I have a friend who gives up saying derogatory things for Lent. She says that at first she finds it terribly difficult. But after trying conscientiously for forty days, she then finds it almost impossible to say anything negative about anybody."

"Why," said my seat companion, "that's a great idea. But for my husband it may be impossible."

"Not if you, yourself, do some of the things we've been talking about," I said. "Not if you really help him."

She laughed. "Not if I do my job as a wife, is that what you mean?"

"That's what I mean," I said.

The seat-belt light had flashed; the plane was beginning its descent into O'Hare airport in Chicago. "You know," my friend said, "it's amazing, really. I mean, hearing your husband preach last Sunday, and then meeting you like this. It's almost as if Somebody or Something planned it this way."

"Who knows?" I said. "Maybe everything that happens is part of a plan."

"Its up to me, now," she said. "I know that. Oh, if I can just get some of this across to my husband!"

"You can," I told her. "There's no reason in the world why you and your husband can't become cheerful, optimistic, outgoing people again. Start thinking that and believing it. Act cheerful and optimistic yourself. Forget about the past with its problems and failures. Live in the present. Make the best possible out of today. Ask God to help and guide you. He will. And since He does, what is there to be gloomy about?"

The big plane settled to the ground with hardly a jolt. Neither of us spoke as we taxied up to the unloading ramp. When the plane finally stopped, my companion drew a long breath. "Thanks," she said. "Thanks for everything. You've set me to thinking. What you have suggested won't be easy, but I really feel excited about trying it. Life can change for both of us. It can be an adventure."

"Good luck," I said, and watched her as she made her way up the aisle and out of sight.

𝒳 7 𝒳

THIS THING
CALLED
GUIDANCE

𝒳 When that lady on the Chicago plane, the one
with the gloomy husband, wondered if perhaps our
meeting was more than just coincidence, she was raising
a very large question—the question of whether there really
is a Supernatural Force or Power that intervenes in human
affairs, sometimes providing answers to problems, sometimes exerting a subtle influence on thought processes,
sometimes arranging or rearranging the complex pattern of
human existence so that desirable goals can be reached.

I firmly believe that there is such a Force and that the
correct name for it is God. I believe that He does indeed
take part in human affairs. I believe that we can ask Him
to do so. And this whole process is something called Guidance.

Norman and I both believe implicitly in the availability
of Divine guidance. We ask for it all the time, in big things
and small, sometimes for ourselves, sometimes for others.
For years, for example, we asked that all three of our children would be guided to marriage partners with whom
they could build strong, happy, successful homes. And those
prayers seem to have been answered. We ask constantly
for guidance in smaller things, too—the little day-to-day
problems that come up all the time. At the Foundation for

Christian Living in Pawling, New York, we have adjoining offices. Often Norman will poke his head into my office or call me on the interoffice phone. "Ruth," he'll say, "there's a decision here that has to be made (or a question that has to be answered, or a letter that needs a carefully worded reply); how about coming in here for a minute? I think we should ask for a little help."

When I go into his office, our technique couldn't be simpler. Norman just talks to the Lord as if He were right there (which we know He is) listening. "Lord," he'll say, "we have this problem. You know what it is without our telling You. Please guide us in the right direction. Make us receptive to Your will. We thank You for this help that You are now giving us."

Then we sit quietly for a while. We don't concentrate furiously on the problem or on possible solutions. We try to make our minds quiet and receptive. Sometimes I will think of some appropriate phrase from the Bible, and focus on that. "Be still, and know that I am God." Or, "In quietness and in confidence shall be your strength." After a while one of us will say to the other, "It seems to me that this is the way to deal with this." Or, "I believe we've been on the wrong track with this one; perhaps we should handle it this way." It's uncanny how often the same conviction will have come to both of us, and how often a clear line of action will open up where things were obscure before.

How can you be sure that you're on the receiving end of guidance? Well, one pretty good indication is when the answer that comes is not the one that you prefer. I think the best example of this in our lives was the time soon after we were married. We were living in Syracuse, New York. Norman was pastor of the University Methodist Church. We were both happy there. We had many friends; things were going extremely well. Then, suddenly, Norman received calls from two very important churches. One was on

the West Coast, in Los Angeles, the largest Methodist congregation in the country. The other came from the Marble
Collegiate Church in New York.

Now, as I have hinted before, one of Norman's basic
characteristics is indecision, a tendency to vacillate, a re-
luctance to make up his mind. I think the chief reason is
that he has a great gift for seeing all sides of a question.
This is a tremendous asset when it comes—say—to counseling a quarreling couple. But it can be a distinct problem in
his own personal life when all sides of the question seem to
cancel out, leaving Norman on dead center, unable to move
in any direction.

This is what happened when the simultaneous calls from
two great churches came in. Actually, there were three possibilities—the third being to refuse both calls and stay where
we were. But there was no doubt that a greater ministry
was awaiting Norman on either the East Coast or the West.
The question was which one to accept.

At first Norman did the natural thing, which was to ask
the advice and counsel of his family, and his friends and
associates in Syracuse. Everyone seemed to have firm
opinions and good reasons to back up those opinions. Norman would listen to one set of arguments and lean in that
direction. Then a conflicting set would be presented, and
he would lean back. He really made up his mind and then
unmade it quite a few times. It was a nerve-wracking
strain not only on him, but on everyone around him. Meantime, time was running out. Both churches wanted an answer.

Finally, I remember, one day after lunch I suggested we
go into our living room. After closing the door I said, "Norman, this can't go on. We're not going to leave this room
until you've come to a decision. And to come to that decision we're going to do what we should have done in the
first place. We're going to put it in God's hands. We're going

to ask for His guidance and wait for it and listen for it until we get it, no matter how long it takes."

We stayed in that room all through the afternoon and far into the evening. I remember we knelt at times by an old chintz-covered couch and held hands and prayed. There were long periods of silence. Norman would pace, and I would sit. We both would turn the pages of the Bible. And no answer seemed to come.

All this time I was quite sure what Norman's preference really was. He wanted to go to California. Many things about it appealed to him. He greatly preferred the climate —Norman hates the hot, humid summers of the East Coast. Some of his best-loved college classmates were there. He liked the simplicity and the openness of the people. He was pleased and flattered by the thought of preaching to what was then the largest Methodist congregation in the country, if not the world. He knew he would be happy in California.

As for New York, he seriously doubted his ability to reach or help a sophisticated Fifth Avenue congregation. He was afraid that his popular approach would be frowned upon by people who expected vast erudition or profound theology. He had heard that the great nave of the Marble Church, capable of seating at least twelve hundred people, seldom had a third that many.

Furthermore, he had been told that Fifth Avenue at 29th Street was a bad location, too far downtown. It was said that industry was moving into that area and residents were moving out. That seemed to mean that the church had nowhere to go but down. Finally, the Marble Church was a different denomination—Reformed Church in America. Norman felt that there were no great theological differences, but he had always been a Methodist, his father was a Methodist minister, there were strong ties of tradition and sentiment to the Methodist Church.

All this was in my mind as we prayed and waited. I knew

it was in Norman's mind too. But we tried as hard as we could to surrender any shred of personal preference and leave the whole thing up to the Lord. We must have said, "Thy will be done" a hundred times, if we said it once.

Finally, I remember, the atmosphere in the room seemed to change. Instead of the uncertainty and urgent seeking, a sudden relaxation of tension came. It was almost as if some great silent clock had struck a deep, decisive note. Norman looked at me and said simply, "Do you have an answer?" "Yes," I said, "I do, but you must make this decision. Have you an answer?"

"I have, indeed," Norman said firmly. "I think God wants us to go to New York." To which I agreed, for the same guidance had come to me.

A few hours before Norman would instantly have cited to me all the good reasons for going to California. But now he seemed sure that New York was where God wanted us.

"In that case," I said, "why don't you pick up the telephone right now and call New York and say you're coming?"

Without a word, he went over to the telephone and put in the long-distance call. Later he told me that all feelings of hesitancy or vacillation were gone. He told the New York official that he would be honored to accept the call to Marble Collegiate Church. Then he sent a telegram to Los Angeles expressing regret that he could not accept their call. After the days of anguished indecision, there was a calmness and a finality about the whole thing that was simply amazing. No sense of frustration or personal disappointment. Just an acceptance of being led, being guided in the right direction.

Was it the right direction? Well, all I can say is that the powerful West Coast church had to struggle with a downtown location, and finally its great edifice was used for other purposes. In the beginning, things were not easy at the Marble Church either—the dead hand of the Depression lay heavy on the city. But gradually the Power that guided us there saw to it that the empty pews were filled to over-flowing, not just once every Sunday morning, but twice, with worshipers in overflow auditoriums watching over closed-circuit television.

Why did God want Norman to go to New York? I can't pretend to know the mind of God, but it seems at least pos-sible to me that God felt that Norman's message of hope and encouragement and spiritual buoyancy was needed more urgently in New York, where the mood of the people was approaching despair, than in California. I think God knew that on weekends in the great impersonal city there were thousands of lonely souls who had nothing to do, no-where to go, young people who needed a place to make friendships, old people who missed the warm religious ties that they had known in smaller communities. We never gave any thought to such considerations when we tried to solve the dilemma with our fallible human minds. But God knew about them all the time.

In the crowded years that have passed since that night in Syracuse I have felt this guidance at work in our lives count-less times. Often it happens right in church on Sunday morning. Time and again, sitting in the pew that I have come to think of as "my" pew, I have heard Norman depart —for no apparent reason—from the outline of his sermon as he had planned to deliver it, depart from it to make a point that just occurs to him "spontaneously," and then after the service have someone come up to me deeply moved. "Mrs. Peale," they'll say, "that point your husband made in his sermon—you know, he must have been talking just to me, because this problem has been a great burden—and now I know what to do about it."

This happens all the time. What is it? Mental telepathy? I don't think so. I think, consciously or unconsciously, the troubled person comes to church seeking guidance. And I think God uses Norman to provide it.

Very often the person being "used" in these guidance situations isn't aware of it at the time. It's only when you look back that the chain of circumstances leading up to the event suddenly seems more planned and more purposeful than mere happenstance.

I remember, for instance, the time we went to dinner with some friends and afterwards saw a household item in their home that interested us. We asked where they got it and were told where such items were sold in Manhattan. "And by the way," they said, "when you go there, ask for Mr. Benton (a fictitious name). He's the young man who sold us this one. He was very obliging and helpful."

A day or two later during lunch hour Norman and I went around to the store and asked for Mr. Benton. We were told that he was out to lunch. Could anyone else help us?

Ordinarily, we might easily have said yes. But this time, for some reason, Norman said we'd come back later. As we left the store I said to him, "Why don't we just look now? What difference does it make who sells it to us?"

"Oh," said Norman vaguely, "this Mr. Benton is a friend of the Morgans'. There may be some small commission in it for him. It won't hurt us to come back. Anyway, I feel I should see him for some reason."

So late in the afternoon, back we went. Now Mr. Benton had gone down to a warehouse to see about a shipment that had just come in. Could anyone else be of service?

This time I was sure that Norman, not always the most patient of men, would buy the item and be done with it. But again he hesitated. "We'd better come back," he told me finally. "Sometimes these things don't perform the way they should once you get them home. I think it would be better to have someone on this end of the transaction who knows some friends of ours, don't you?"

"You can come back if you like," I said a bit crossly. "I've really got too much to do to keep running in and out of this store looking for Mr. Benton!"

So two days later Norman went back alone. This time he found Mr. Benton in his office. He was a handsome young man, but harassed-looking. "Mr. Benton," Norman said, "my name is Peale. I'm interested in buying your item. You sold one like it to some friends of ours, the Morgans. They sent me."

"I know who you are, Dr. Peale," the young man said quietly. "But the Morgans didn't send you."

"They didn't?" said Norman, taken aback.

"No," said Mr. Benton, "God sent you. I'm on the verge of killing myself because I don't deserve to live. I planned to do it last weekend. Then I decided to wait one more week—this week—and ask God one more time to send me help. And here you are."

Norman got up, walked over to the door, closed it. "Tell me about it," he said.

The young man poured out a tragic story about an involvement with his best friend's wife. The friend was in Viet-Nam. The girl had become pregnant. Overwhelmed by guilt and remorse, she had committed suicide. Now her lover felt that he should impose the same punishment on himself. It was one of those poignant and devastating situations that ministers are so often called upon to face.

Calling on all his experience, all his understanding of fallible human beings, all his spiritual insight, Norman was able to bring a measure of peace to the tormented young man and eventually help him start rebuilding his shattered life.

But what brought about that meeting in the first place? What impelled Norman to keep trying until he actually came face to face with the young man? Was it just coincidence? Mr. Benton certainly didn't think so. I don't either. A soul in torment cried out for help, and that help was *guided* to it.

In seeking for guidance, it certainly helps if you are a

religious person consciously turning to God. But I believe the power can work even with nonreligious people, if their objective is a morally valid one and if they will just subdue their own egos and listen. Some years ago I remember reading a book by Major General J. B. Medaris, who was in command of our national space effort in the early days at Huntsville, Alabama. The Russians had put up their first satellite, Sputnik I, and tremendous pressure was on the Army to get an American satellite into orbit quickly. In those days, Medaris was not a devoutly religious person at all; he was a tough, hard-boiled soldier. But he wrote that often when a critical decision had to be made—and there were dozens every day—he would turn away from his staff of advisers, go to a window and stand there, staring out at the landscape and just *waiting*. Invariably, he said, an answer would come into his head. And almost always—far too often to be explained by mere human intelligence or experience—the answer was the right one. Less than one hundred days after Sputnik, Explorer I was in the heavens.

Was that guidance? I'm sure it was. And I'm pretty sure General Medaris came to think so too, because after his retirement from the Army, stricken by cancer, he experienced a recovery so miraculous and inexplicable by medical standards that he decided to enter the ministry and is now an ordained Episcopal priest.

Another form of guidance that I have come to believe in might be called "closed door" guidance. There are certainly times in every life when hopes are not realized, when ambitions fail, when plans don't work out the way you think they should. Quite often this is simple cause-and-effect; you didn't look ahead, you didn't work hard enough, your timing was wrong, you antagonized someone. In such cases, the disappointment is probably your own fault.

But there are also times when things seem to go wrong without any mistakes or lack of effort on your part, almost of their own accord. When this happens in my life, I've learned to ask myself if that particular door has swung shut because the Lord has closed it. I have also come to believe that if the Lord closes one door in your face, it may easily be because He intends to open a better one for you later on.

Time and again in my life I have had to accept what seemed like a defeat or a frustration at the time, only to realize later that it was actually to my advantage. Giving up my sophomore year in college in Detroit and going to work at the telephone company to help my brother through his senior year was a case in point. As I've already related, I was unhappy and resentful because I thought my carefully planned college timetable was being upset. But actually my whole future life-pattern hinged on that delay, because without it I would never have met Norman. As I said in an earlier chapter, I would almost certainly have left Syracuse before he arrived there.

Norman's mother was also a firm believer in this sort of guidance that seems negative at the time but becomes triumphantly positive in the end. She used to say—and I can still hear her clear, confident voice saying it—"If a door seems to close in your face, and you can't get it open, it means that God has shut that door because He wants to guide you to another door somewhere down the line. And if you go down the line and find a lot of closed doors, that means He doesn't want you to go into any of those places or situations. Just keep on going, and eventually you'll find a door that is open to you because it is right for you."

Many famous people have had this experience. One summer in Switzerland, Norman and I met the well-known novelist, A. J. Cronin, who wrote *The Keys of the Kingdom*, *The Stars Look Down*, and many other best sellers. He told us how he had started out in life as a medical doctor in London's fashionable West End. He became one of the most successful young physicians in Harley Street, making a great deal of money.

One reason he made money, Cronin told us with amazing candor, was that the bulk of his time was spent reassuring and fussing over rich hypochondriacs, most of whom weren't really sick at all, but were willing to pay large fees just to have Cronin practice his comforting bedside manner on them.

Cronin said he was uneasy about this state of affairs, but he kept on with it anyway—until suddenly the door that led to the type of medicine he was practicing slammed shut. He developed gastric ulcers and was told to take a long rest. He went home to Scotland where he spent six months in a bleak, rain-swept highland village.

At first he was deeply despondent and depressed about his medical career, which seemed finished. But then, he told us, he began to hear voices of dimly perceived characters saying, "Bring us to life. Put us down on paper."

So Cronin, who had no experience in writing at all, began struggling with a book. He found it hideously hard work. At one point he became so discouraged that he threw his whole manuscript into the ash can. (My husband did the same thing with *his* first major book manuscript.) But an old Scotsman persuaded him to dig it out and try again. The result, in the end, was Cronin's brilliantly successful first novel: *Hatter's Castle*. A new door had opened in his life. But if the other door hadn't been closed to him, he would never have sought for and finally found the right one. And Cronin was deeply grateful.

Norman's father, Charles Clifford Peale, had a somewhat similar experience, except that when he turned from medicine it was not to writing. Again it was a serious illness at the age of twenty-five that brought about—or seemed to bring about—the change. Up to that point he had been a highly respected physician—Health Commissioner, in fact, for a midwestern city. But when he recovered from his illness, he found that his interest in practicing medicine was gone. He felt a strong conviction that God had spared his life so that he might serve Him more directly, as a minister. One door had closed, another had opened. He went into the ministry where he spent the remainder of a long and useful life.

This whole business of guidance, obviously, is a highly personal thing. No one can prove to anyone else that it exists. All I can do is recommend to anyone who is troubled or uncertain or confused that they ask for it—and see what happens.

It's a free gift, but you have to be willing to accept a gift before you can receive it. And believe me, it helps greatly in the adventure of being a wife.

Let me tell you of one night that Norman and I will never forget.

It was a Sunday that had been a happy day from morning until night, and then—! After church we went to lunch with some friends and had a relaxed and enjoyable visit. The day was, you might say, one grand, sweet song. In the afternoon we did some other interesting things and finally got home about seven P.M. to find a message to call a surgeon at the North Carolina University Hospital in Chapel Hill.

Our son, John, was completing his studies for a doctorate of philosophy degree at the university. We made the call. The surgeon said, "Your son came into this hospital today in an emergency, suffering great agony. We've tested him throughout the afternoon and we've arrived at a diagnosis of inflamed gallbladder with probable pancreatic complications." He continued, "We're medicating him, trying to delay operating, because he has a hot gallbladder [that's what he called it]. It's dangerous to operate with the gallbladder in this condition. We hope to reduce the infection and bring down his temperature first and operate on him later."

"Well, doctor," I said, "he is in your hands and he is in God's hands. You do what you think is best." We immediately went into prayer, praying for the doctor, praying for our only son. At 11:15 that night the doctor called back and said, "John hasn't responded to medication. The situation is becoming very serious. I do not like to operate under these conditions—it's dangerous to operate; but it's more dangerous not to. So I must operate."

Again I said, "Doctor, he is in your hands and in God's hands. Dr. Peale and I will be with you in prayer. Bring him through for us."

"I'll try mighty hard," he said.

So then we faced each other. This is our only son. We knew he was in great danger. But all our lives we have practiced to the best of our ability the idea of letting go and letting God. But it is very hard to let go of your own son when everything within you draws him to yourself, but I believe we achieved it.

The doctor had said he would call us back in about two to three hours, that being the time he thought the operation would require.

But he didn't call us back. Four hours passed; then five hours. Six hours went by. We literally prayed all night long. Even though no word had come from the surgeon, at about 3:30 in the morning I had a strong conviction that it was going to be all right with John and that I could leave him in the hands of God. I told this to Norman. He said, "I had the same feeling a few moments ago."

At six o'clock in the morning the doctor called. He said, "I'm glad to report that John came through the operation successfully. He's a very sick boy, but he is also a good healthy boy. He has lived a clean life, and that counts when the chips are down. I feel that he will be all right."

Not in years have I had so great a sense of the greatness and the goodness and the love of God as I did that night.

Later I learned that at about three A.M. the situation became so serious that they brought the hospital's chief surgeon in to take part in the operation. I also told the doctor I had been praying for my son all night. He said, "I always try to work in partnership with God."

In this deeply human crisis, which occurs in every family in one form or another, we learned once again that you can trust this thing called guidance.

8

HELICOPTER
FLIGHT TO
THE MATTERHORN

For a small-town Ohio boy and small-town Iowa girl, Norman and I have been very fortunate, for we have seen a good deal of the world. World travel is just about our favorite pastime. As a very young man, only three years out of seminary and still single, Norman financed his first trip to Europe by acting as tour guide for a party of tourists, mostly very eligible young ladies. His mother was afraid that some designing member of the party might lure him into matrimony, but he managed to come through it without any entangling alliances. And the glimpses he got of other places and people were so enticing that he's been traveling ever since. We have crossed the Atlantic forty times and the Pacific eight times. And we've been twice around the world.

Most of our foreign travel takes place in the summer when Norman can relinquish his pulpit for three months. But these trips are not just for pleasure. Norman works constantly, wherever he is. Most of his books have been written during these so-called vacations. One summer we rented a chalet on the Bürgenstock above Lake Lucerne in Switzerland and worked eight hours every day; he writing, I editing and typing and retyping. When the creativity bogged down, we would go on long walks in the mountains, always returning with renewed vigor and inspiration. Another summer in the Holy Land we took along a photographer and did endless research to write the book, *Adventures in the Holy Land*.

If there isn't a book under contract, there are always newspaper columns or magazine articles to write, manuscripts to edit, sermons to be outlined, people to see. Norman really hates to be idle; a friend of his once said that he has "a lust for work." He's really incapable of sustained loafing. Unless he feels that he's accomplishing something, he's miserable.

I must confess that, to a degree, I'm the same way. So we get a lot of work done. But we also try to find time for recreation in the literal sense of the word. We love to read. (Norman can easily read a book a day, which frustrates me because I'm so much slower.) We go to the opera and concerts; we mingle among the people wherever we are. (I take a subway ride in every city that has one, and ride the buses whenever possible.) We go to a baseball game in Tokyo, for instance, rather than a reception. We go sightseeing only to those places we find important after studying the area from an historical point of view. We try to find periods of quietness, of withdrawal, of inspiration, where the batteries can be recharged.

This is not something that you can command; you can't leap up in the morning and announce, "Today we're going to get our creativity renewed." It's a more subtle thing. We try not to be regimented or harassed by schedules so that we can take a quiet walk or expose ourselves to the majesty of the mountains or the vastness of the sea. Or watch a sunrise or tramp a country road in the rain. In other words, we aim to make ourselves as receptive as possible to the lifeforce that surrounds and sustains us all.

But perhaps the greatest benefit in travel is the stimulus of novelty. As you move about, you meet new people, encounter new ideas, observe new customs, hear new stories. For Norman and me, these experiences are not only stimulating in themselves, they supply the raw material that Norman draws on for radio talks and sermons, lectures and newspaper columns all through the winter months. Many people, I'm sure, think of a writer or a preacher as someone who, like a kind of human spider, spins his webs out of some magical and inexhaustible reservoir inside him. But this isn't so. You have to take in something before you can send it back out. The creative process that receives this "something" reshapes it, gives it form and substance and drama. But there has to be a steady input, or the well will run dry.

Of course, you never know whether or not a given day will offer a memorable experience. But you know that any day might, and so you live in a state of constant anticipation. I think sometimes that this capacity for eager expectation is the secret of Norman's amazing youthfulness. He's always willing to try anything, go anywhere, talk to anybody. Both his parents were the same way. His mother had tremendous intellectual energy and curiosity. His father, who was a medical doctor before he became a minister, had an endless series of interests: politics, astronomy, the Civil War—even snakes! He was a real expert on reptiles. So Norman gets the precious gift of enthusiasm from both sides.

To give you an idea of what travel and new experiences do for us, let me describe a single morning from a trip last summer. In our travels over the years we have visited some wonderful places and seen some unforgettable sights. But I think perhaps the hour we spent between eleven A.M. and noon last August 12, for sheer visual excitement and spiritual impact, topped them all.

We were in Zermatt, a little town in Switzerland that nestles in a valley at the foot of the Matterhorn. This gigantic spire of jagged granite looks like a great knife thrust into the sky. The summit is more than 14,000 feet above sea level. Not far away is the Monte Rosa, highest mountain in Switzerland, but its approaches are more gradual and it's not so dramatic. The Matterhorn stands alone, brooding, sombre, pockmarked even in summer with ice and snow. For years the natives believed that it was the home of devils or evil spirits who could hurl thunderbolts or fling down great boulders upon any humans who dared to come close. Someone once said that the Matterhorn isn't just a mountain; it's a "presence." It is.

This "presence" and the town of Zermatt have been linked in the minds of mountaineers everywhere for over a century. In the year 1864 a young Englishman named Edward Whymper came to Zermatt. Climbing the Matterhorn was an obsession with him. In previous summers he had made several attempts that ended in failure. Now, spurred on by the knowledge that a team of Italian climbers was preparing an assault on the mountain from the south, he put together a hastily organized seven-man party consisting of four guides and two other young Englishmen, one of whom was little more than a beginner.

Somehow this makeshift team made it to the summit of the great mountain. But on the way back down, one of the Englishmen slipped. The party was roped together, but for some reason the rope they were using was the weakest one they had—little more than a length of sash cord. The falling man dragged three of the others with him. One of the guides tried to check their terrible slide toward a precipice, but the inadequate rope broke and they plunged over the edge. Horrified and shaken, Whymper and the two remaining guides completed the descent to Zermatt. The other four were dead.

In Zermatt there is a little museum full of reminders of that tragic day so long ago: photographs, newspaper accounts, equipment, even a piece of the fatal rope itself. The tragedy had enormous impact on Victorian England. Many voices were raised condemning mountaineering as an insane and unnatural sport. But the publicity just brought more climbers to Zermatt. Today the approaches are so well-known that during the summer months dozens of climbers scale the mountain each week. Even so, there are still falls, and sometimes fatalities.

During our visit to Zermatt last summer we stayed in the chalet of an old friend, Theodore Seiler, a Swiss banker and president of the Seiler Hotels. Ted Seiler grew up in Zermatt. His grandfather owned the first hotel there, the Monte Rosa, where Ted still welcomes guests. It was to this hotel that Whymper returned from his triumphant but tragic climb. A bronze plaque near the entrance commemorates the event.

Ted Seiler told us that, next to climbing the Matterhorn, the most dramatic way to view it was to fly around it and over it in a helicopter. He added that a pair of helicopters, flown by German pilots, was kept on the alert at all times on the outskirts of Zermatt. There was a small one that could carry four persons, and a larger one that could take six. They had already made several highly dramatic mountain rescues. Ted Seiler said that if the weather was right, he might be able to arrange for us to make a mountain flight over the nearby peaks and glaciers. He said that if we did, we'd never forget it.

It sounded exciting, all right, but also a little scary. I had been in a helicopter only once in my life, to view some farm acreage. But Norman, on the trip he made to Viet Nam at the request of President Nixon, had made many helicopter flights. Some of these took him across jungle areas controlled by the Viet Cong. On one such trip, his escort was an Army general. As they flew along, Norman noticed the soldier's lips moving silently. "Are you praying, General?" he asked half-jokingly. "Sure," replied the General promptly. "Aren't you?"

We were only staying in Zermatt for six days. All through

the first part of our visit, the weather was uncertain. Much of the time swirling clouds shrouded the Matterhorn. When they would part momentarily, we could see that the slopes around the great peak were covered with fresh snow. But the pinnacle itself was too steep for much snow to cling to the jagged rocks.

The night before our last day in Zermatt, the wind switched to the north—a sign of fair weather, Ted Seiler said. Sure enough, the next day dawned sparkling and bright. The sky was a deep, cobalt blue—not a cloud in it. Golden sunlight poured down on the streets of Zermatt, gay with banners and colored awnings and window boxes full of petunias and geraniums. No automobiles are allowed in Zermatt, so vehicles are horse-drawn. The big hotel vans are pulled by matched pairs of horses, handsome grays or chestnuts, with bells on their harnesses. They clatter down the narrow main street to meet every train. Now and then a herd of goats trots through the town, the bells around their necks jangling musically. Tourists skip out of their way, or whip out their cameras: sunburned Germans in shorts, their ice-axes protruding from their rucksacks; French and Italians, English and Americans, even a handful of energetic Japanese, all drawn by the great magnet of the Matterhorn.

A telephone call was made to the heliport, a square of concrete built into a hillside just above the railroad tracks on the north side of the town. We were told that if we would come there at eleven o'clock, there was a good chance that we could make the flight. The big helicopter was undergoing repairs, but the small one was operational. Since there would be room for three passengers in addition to the pilot, a writer friend of ours who was also in Zermatt said he would like to go.

It was a ten-minute walk to the tall, silo-like structure that housed the elevator that lifted visitors to the heliport. We pressed a button, identified ourselves through a transmitter like the ones you see in the lobbies of apartment houses, and shortly found ourselves standing on a huge square of concrete about half the size of a football field. A painted circle with a large H in the center was evidently the target for descending pilots. Through the open doors of a hangar we could see the large red machine being worked on. We were told that the smaller helicopter was off on patrol, but would return shortly.

The manager of the heliport brought three chairs, and we sat in the brilliant sunshine, waiting. I don't know about the others, but my feelings were a mixture of excitement, anticipation, and a little apprehension at the thought of soaring off the friendly earth in a plastic bubble supported by nothing but a pair of ungainly windmill blades and a single engine.

As we waited, we talked about Whymper and mountain climbing and the strange and dangerous things people seem to do in their quest for happiness. Our writer friend asked us what activity made *us* happiest. Norman said that he was happiest when, in the middle of a talk or sermon, he felt that he was really communicating, reaching his audience in a helpful or inspiring way. "It's a wonderful feeling," he said. "There's nothing quite like it." I said that I thought I was happiest when, in a group mulling over some problem or dilemma, I was suddenly able to see a valid solution and point it out. The sense of achievement that came from solving difficulties, I said, even minor ones, was very gratifying.

Our friend said that he was happiest when he was least conscious of himself—and that was usually when he was doing something out-of-doors that required a degree of skill: tennis, hunting, fishing. He added that he couldn't enjoy this, though, unless he had earned it by doing a certain amount of work. Norman laughed. "I know what you mean," he said. "There's happiness in all these things. But maybe in the last analysis the happiest people are the ones who're doing what they think God wants them to do."

Our ears picked up the pulsing drone of the helicopter before our eyes saw it. Then suddenly there it was, hovering like a gigantic dragonfly. The pilot swung around into the wind. With a roar and buffeting gusts of the cool mountain air, the machine settled onto the concrete platform. The pilot cut the engine. The whirling blades gradually ceased revolving and grew still.

The fuel tanks were refilled. Certain mountain-rescue equipment was taken out to make room for us. Almost before we knew what was happening, Norman and I were fastening our seatbelts in the rear seat. Our friend sat forward, on the left. The young pilot, relaxed and self-assured, was on the right. "Do we speak German or English?" he asked politely.

"English," he was told.

"Where do you want to go?"

At this the station manager standing on the pad spoke to the pilot through his open window. It was in German and I could not understand, but a resistance on the part of the pilot and then a shrug of the shoulder by the pilot as the station manager insisted, gave me a tremor of apprehension. Was he being asked to push this helicopter beyond its limit in order to show us the glorious mountain?

The doors swung shut. The pilot adjusted his earphones and spoke a few words in German to the controller inside the hangar. His right hand held the stick. With his left, he twisted the throttle between the two forward seats. The helicopter vibrated, stirred, began to lift. Suddenly, with a heart-stopping lurch, it seemed to me that we simply jumped off the concrete platform into thin air. There was no forward taxiing, as in a conventional aircraft. We leaned into the wind—and leaped!

Up the little valley we rushed, not more than two hundred feet off the ground. The pilot and the passenger in the front seat could see almost straight down; I was glad we couldn't. On the instrument panel I could see the air-speed indicator; the needle was hovering between forty and fifty knots. The altimeter indicated that we were about six thousand feet above sea level, and climbing.

Up the valley we flew, between towering rock walls on either side, past lacy waterfalls, over green meadows filled with mountain wild flowers. The helicopter banked steeply and started back, still climbing.

Below us, now, we could see Zermatt spread out like a toy village, its chalets and hotels dominated by the spire of the church. We were following the contours of the ground to the east of the town. Once or twice it seemed to me that our rate of climb was too slow to enable us to clear the ridge just ahead, but we always slid over with something to spare. Far below I could see the orange cars of a funicular crawling along, like ladybugs, between pylons. Now the dark hues of the evergreens were giving way to the browns and grays of the rugged terrain above the timberline. Ahead and to the left was a cluster of buildings marking the terminus of the cog railway that climbs steeply up from Zermatt to Gornergrat, some ten thousand feet above sea level, a favorite lookout point for tourists who want to view the whole majestic panorama of glaciers and Alpine peaks.

But few tourists ever saw them as we were seeing them now. Moments later we were over the Gorner-glacier itself, a huge river of ice, blinding white, strangely scored and indented. Where it ended, a torrent of water, gray with glacial sediment, poured from under the wall of ice. To our right, a lordly peak, the Stockhorn, pierced the sky. The altimeter now read eleven thousand feet, and some dim unwelcome memory reminded me that as a rule pilots are not supposed to fly above ten thousand without oxygen. We had no oxygen.

Up the glacier we raced at sixty knots. Tortured and barren as the ridged ice was, I was glad to have it there, only a couple of hundred feet below. If our engine stopped, I told myself cheerfully, we could just sit down on that nice solid ice and wait to be rescued—perhaps by a friendly St. Bernard. But then, looking ahead, I saw that the glacier ended. And not just the glacier, but the mountain, the world, creation ended. Rushing toward us was a fine white line, sharp as a knife blade. Then nothing. Just a kind of livid emptiness.

Over the line we went, straight out into this awful chasm. I felt my feet pressing against the floor, as if by doing so they could somehow hold us back. Beneath us the precipice fell sheer, straight down, for more than a mile. We hung suspended over a stupendous void, ringed by the great peaks, floored by purple shadow.

I grabbed Norman's hand. "Ruth, are you nervous?" he asked, surprised, for it takes a lot to trouble me.

"Oh, no," I answered feebly, "just excited!"

My rational mind knew that we could fly just as well over a mile of nothingness as over a glacier, but my stomach didn't seem to know it. My stomach, in fact, seemed to have stayed back over the glacier. I saw that our writer friend had reached for the side of our plastic bubble as if to brace himself, and I knew he too was wondering what four infinitesimally small and unimportant human beings were doing in such a sublimely terrifying place.

Only the pilot seemed unconcerned. We swung behind the twin peaks of the Monte Rosa, still higher than our heads although our altimeter now indicated twelve thousand feet. Below us a few ants seemed to be toiling painfully across the vast snowfields. Climbers. "That can be dangerous," said the pilot, pointing at them, "unless you know what you're doing. There are snow bridges that can break.

See those holes that look like caves? If you fall in one of those, you're finished. No one can get you out!"

He spotted something lying on the crest of one of the ridges, something that might have been a man lying in the snow. "Better take a look." The helicopter banked steeply; the rotor blades made a flat, thudding sound as they bit into the air. I clutched Norman's hand with even greater fervor. "Just a tent," said the pilot as we swept over the object. "Sometimes climbers will try the Monte Rosa one day and the Matterhorn the next, and spend the night down there." I tried to imagine what it would be like underneath that tiny piece of canvas with the wind moaning in the icy blackness outside. My imagination wasn't up to it.

Now we were over a high plateau where hundreds of skiers had gathered, eleven thousand feet up, for summer skiing. You could see them queued up for the ski lift, or sweeping down the broad white slopes. "That's the Plateau Rosa," the pilot said. "Most of those skiers come up from the Italian side. Now let's take a look at the Matterhorn."

The Matterhorn is impressive at a distance. Close up, it is overpowering. And we were close, so close that it seemed to me we could see the cracks in the towering walls. But when the pilot pointed out some climbers, they looked unbelievably tiny, just dots of color clinging to the naked rock. Past a small hut we went, perched like an eagle's nest on the edge of a stupendous precipice. "Climbers spend the night there," the pilot said. "They start climbing at dawn."

We were still climbing ourselves, in a tight spiral that circled the Matterhorn three times. It seemed to me that our engine was laboring in the thin air. I was beginning to feel some shortness of breath, and I could see that Norman was too. Now the altimeter read fourteen thousand feet; we were almost on a level with the summit. I could see clearly the iron cross that marked the spot where Whymper and his companions had stood so long ago. Higher still, so that we could look down on the summit itself. There on that dizzying height, three tiny figures stood, waving at us, and I felt a sudden surge of admiration for the restless, unquenchable spirit of adventure that had made them challenge and conquer those frowning heights. Perhaps our generation was not so soft and effete after all.

Then we were dropping down through the luminous air, the great mountain receding behind us. "Swallow hard," the pilot said. "It will ease the pressure on your ears." Zermatt came into view, tranquil in the sunlight. The landing pad looked like a linen handkerchief. We made one last turn, came up into the wind, settled down exactly in the center of the painted circle. The flight was over.

Our friend Ted Seiler had arranged for the hotel van to meet us. The two splendid horses trotted back to the village, bells jingling gaily. We sat in the old coach—it had been old when he was a boy, Ted Seiler said—not saying much. The spell of the heights was still on us, and the transition from twentieth-century helicopter to nineteenth-century horse-drawn van was so abrupt and so strange that it seemed unreal.

All through the rest of that day, and many times since, I have found myself reliving the exaltation of that moment when we swept over the edge of the glacier into that vast emptiness, and the thought has come to me that perhaps dying is like that: an outward rush into the unknown where there is nothing recognizable, nothing to cling to, and yet you are sustained and supported over the great void just as you were over the comfortable and familiar terrain.

Fanciful? Perhaps. But I remember that when we said our prayers that night, thanking God for the privilege of seeing all we had seen, and also for our safe return, it didn't seem fanciful. Not at all.

🌿 9 🌿

WHEN IN-LAWS
BECOME
OUTLAWS

🌿 The pretty young wife seemed both apprehensive and angry. "Mrs. Peale," she said, "my husband's mother is coming to visit us next week. She's going to stay ten days—ten whole days! And I can't stand it!"

She had approached me in the aisle of the church following the second Sunday morning church service. She identified herself as a member of the church's Young Adult group. Her problem, she said, was one she couldn't discuss dispassionately with her husband. Could she ask me about it?

"Of course," I said, and she told me about the imminent visit of her mother-in-law. "I just can't stand it!" she repeated, and actually stamped her well-shod little foot.

"What is there about it that you can't stand?" was the question I asked her.

"I can't stand the way she tries to manage everything," she said. "From the moment she comes into our house, she just takes over. She has tremendous energy. She's a very positive sort of person. So the way I prepare the meals isn't right; she always knows a better way. My housekeeping isn't well-organized; she keeps telling me to do it differently. No matter how I handle the children, she always has other ideas. By the time she's been in the house twenty-four hours, I feel as if it were no longer mine, but hers. She's my husband's mother, and I know I'm supposed to love her, but, Mrs. Peale, this woman drives me right up the wall."

Then she continued a little more calmly, "She's a widow, and Jack is her only son, so I can't refuse to have her visit us occasionally. But it causes so much friction between Jack and me that sometimes I think we'll get in the habit of fighting. And that is bad. What on earth can I do?"

I knew that Norman had scheduled a meeting with his officers to discuss some church matters, so I had a few minutes to spare. "Let's sit over here in the corner of this pew and talk about it," I said. "There are some remedies for this problem of yours. You might find it exciting to try some of them."

It's practically universal, this in-law problem. Very few married couples escape it entirely. Norman and I had our share of it too. We were devoted to each other's parents, but we found them trying at times. Norman felt that my mother was rigid and uncompromising, with little tolerance or understanding of people whose views or standards differed from her own. I had to admit that this was true. On the other hand, I felt that his mother, gifted though she was, could be domineering and possessive. And determined to have her own way.

For example, when we were first married, we always had to go to Mother Peale's home for Christmas. "I may not be here next year," she would say plaintively if I suggested going to my parents or wanted to make other plans. So we always wound up going there . . . and I always had to control and mask my resentment.

Both of us got along better with our fathers-in-law than we did with our mothers-in-law. This also seems to be the general rule; the sharp-edged jokes about in-laws are seldom directed at men. Perhaps this is because fathers are less inclined than mothers to judge or criticize the person their child chooses to marry. Or perhaps their interests are focused on their jobs and not so much on personal relationships. In any case, fathers-in-law seldom seem to generate the kind of friction that mothers-in-law do.

Norman and I were lucky in that from the start we agreed to discuss our feelings about the other's parents openly and honestly—in private. We agreed not to get angry or defensive when the subject of in-laws came up, but to treat it as a kind of good-humored verbal pillow-fight in which either of us could say anything within reason and not do any damage to the fabric of our own marriage.

And it was amazing how often the appraisal voiced was accurate, but never admitted by either of us to ourselves previously. There is always that fine line of fearing disloyalty. But such openness between Norman and me always brought us closer together and made for a depth of understanding that was a great experience every time it happened.

"Your mother's so darn narrow-minded," Norman would complain. "Why does she have to object to my father's cigars? When she sees him light one, she acts as if she had found him breaking all the Ten Commandments at once. What business is it of hers? Why don't you tell her to cut it out?"

"What she really objects to," I'd reply with some asperity, "is that sometimes when your father's cigars don't taste right, he spits in the fireplace! Why don't you tell him to cut *that* out?"

Or I might say, "Why is your mother so full of fears and phobias about things? She's always sure that the worst is going to happen. She sees a disaster around every corner. I don't want this kind of timidity to rub off on my children the way it did on your brothers and you!"

"My mother's *not* timid!" Norman would counter. "She has a vivid imagination, that's all. At times she thinks you can be pretty callous. She told me that when she was with you in the park the other day, and John fell off his tricycle, you didn't even pick him up. You let some stranger passing by do it!"

"That's right," I'd say. "I knew he wasn't hurt. I wanted him to pick himself up. Your mother acted as if he had broken both arms and legs. That's just what I'm talking about!"

So we'd say to each other anything that came to mind, and I think it was the best possible form of ventilation. I also think that we each secretly wanted the other to defend his parents with fire and sword. After all, a person who doesn't love his parents isn't likely to have much love-capacity in him for a married partner or anyone else.

In talking with a young couple a few days before their marriage, I happened to mention that one of the greatest arts they would have to learn as man and wife was to talk together about each other's parents with absolute honesty and openness. The bride-to-be seemed startled and unbelieving. "Do you really mean that, Mrs. Peale?" she asked.

"Of course I do," I replied. "In fact, I think it's an absolute necessity for harmony and understanding between any husband and wife."

Sally turned to Jim. She held back as though in doubt and then asked, "Jim, do you think we can do that?"

He hesitated, and in a flash I knew that inadvertently I had stumbled onto the thing that could be their greatest problem. He looked at her thoughtfully. It was a long moment, and I almost saw him grow up before my very eyes. I could actually feel the hold his mother had on him. Then he said, "Honey, let's do it! Will you help me?"

Over the years, Norman and I have seen more than one marriage founder under the impact of the in-law problem. We have also seen cases where marriages were prevented by pressures exerted by a possessive parent, usually the mother. In one strange case a young woman who had spent her twenties and early thirties looking after a supposedly invalid mother came to Norman after the old lady died. She explained that she had never married because her mother needed her. But now she was haunted by a terrible fear—fear that her mother had been buried alive.

It was one of those cases where the fear is so irrational and so deep that ordinary religious counseling is of little value. Fortunately the psychiatrists at the American Foundation of Religion and Psychiatry were able to help the girl. One of these doctors told Norman later that the girl's irrational dread was actually a disguised fear that her mother might not be really dead, that she might still come back from the grave to dominate and warp and twist her daughter's life. It took long and patient therapy to rid the young woman of her morbid obsession.

There was another instance where a young wife came to Norman and told him that she was going to have to divorce her husband. None of the usual reasons for such an attitude seemed to exist. Finally it came out that her mother had disapproved violently of the marriage. "If you marry that man against my wishes," she said ominously to her daughter, "it will be the death of me!" Sure enough, soon after the wedding—which she refused to attend—the old dragon had a heart attack and died. This set up such profound guilt feelings in the daughter's unconscious mind that she came to feel that she could atone for her mother's death only by divorcing her husband. "My mother may be dead," she sobbed, "but her influence isn't. I can still feel her surrounding me, pressuring me. The only way I'll ever be rid of her condemnation is by divorcing my husband. Then maybe she'll let me alone!"

Sometimes Norman's instincts tell him that the best way to deal with an emotional problem is to be brusque. He said to his tormented visitor, "Listen to me. You are now a married woman. You are supposed to be a mature person. You must stop acting like a frightened child. Your mother is no longer here. She's gone. She's dead. To get rid of these feelings that are troubling you, you don't have to divorce a perfectly good husband. All you have to do is repeat these words after me: 'Mother, you cannot dominate me any longer. You have no control over me. I am living. You are dead. I hereby *command* you to take your cold, dead hand off my life!' "

"Oh, Dr. Peale," the young woman gasped. "I couldn't say a thing like that!"

"Say it!" Norman insisted. "Say it and be free!"

Finally she said it, and such is the power of suggestion that from that moment she *was* free, and was troubled no longer.

Sometimes it takes more than the power of suggestion to control a rampaging maternal instinct. Not long ago a friend of ours told us of a conversation he had with a distinguished California jurist, Judge Alton B. Pfaff. Judge Pfaff, who for years presided over a Court of Domestic Relations in Los Angeles, told of a case where a young soldier appealed to him for help. The boy had married a girl who was completely dominated by her mother. She could make no move, no decision without consulting Mom. Everything had to be reported to Mom. Everything had to be approved by Mom.

To a certain type of personality, exercising this sort of power over another person is morbidly satisfying, and Mom had no intention of relinquishing it. At first she insisted that the newlyweds live in her house, where she watched every move with an eagle eye. The son-in-law, naturally, was miserable. Finally he moved himself and his bride into a small apartment, but even there the mother-in-law followed them, appearing uninvited at all hours, sometimes persuading the bride to go back and spend the night with her instead of with her husband.

Finally, to his vast relief, the young soldier was transferred to Arizona. He took his bride with him, and set about starting a new life. But one day he came home to find that his mother-in-law had flown to Arizona, had persuaded her daughter that she was unhappy there, and had actually taken her back to California. It was at this point that the husband, returning to Los Angeles in search of his wife, appealed to Judge Pfaff.

The Judge settled the matter by issuing a court order directing the mother-in-law to stop interfering in the marriage and forbidding her to set foot in her son-in-law's house without an invitation issued by him. She was warned that to violate the order would place her in contempt and bring swift and punitive action from the court. So she didn't dare to disobey it. But it took the full power of the judicial system to make her stop wrecking her daughter's life.

In yet another case that we know of, a woman who was a good Christian and a pillar of her church developed a painful limp. No physical cause for it could be discovered; she simply went lame. Her pastor, a wise man, had recently performed the wedding ceremony for this woman's daughter. He knew that she had disapproved of the marriage and deeply resented her new son-in-law.

In a long talk with the woman, the minister told her that he thought her limp might well be the reflection of a twisted condition in her mind. "I'm afraid you're guilty of sin," he said, "the sin of despising another human being. I believe you hate your son-in-law, although he has done nothing to deserve your condemnation. I believe you have this limp because something deep within you knows that you are not walking uprightly in your heart, and so you can't walk uprightly in your everyday life."

The woman's eyes filled with tears. "You may be right," she said. "What can I do?"

"I want you to come to the church with me," the pastor said, "and kneel at the altar. I want you to confess this sin of anger and hatred, and ask for release and forgiveness. I want you to take Communion and resolve to make a fresh start. Then I want you to go to your son-in-law and admit your fault and ask for his forgiveness too. I believe that if you will do the first few things, the last will not be so hard."

Actually, it was very hard, but the woman did it. She went to the nearby town where her daughter and son-in-law lived. She rang the doorbell. When her son-in-law came to the door, she managed a tremulous smile. "I'm your wicked mother-in-law," she said, "come to ask your forgiveness for many things."

He was a perceptive young man. He didn't say a word. He just gave her a hug and drew her into the house. From that point on, they were friends. And the minister must have been right about the limp, because it disappeared.

Norman has a somewhat similar mother-in-law story that he loves to tell about the man whose mother-in-law lived in the same house. The man came to Norman claiming that she was driving him crazy, not because she was interfering or domineering, but because she was ruining his breakfasts. Every morning, he said, he liked to get up and have a cup of coffee alone in the kitchen. But every morning his mother-in-law would come scuffing downstairs in an old bathrobe with curlers in her hair and heelless slippers on her feet which made a horrible dragging sound when she walked. She never said anything worth listening to. She would pour herself a cup of coffee and drink it with loud slurping sounds. Like a horse, the man said. And not only that, but when she sat at the table she would maddeningly scrunch her toast. One more scrunch, the man said, one more slurp, and he was going to commit murder . . . or else leave his own home for good.

"Well," Norman said to him, "I can give you a solution to your problem. But I doubt if you're brave enough to attempt it."

"Try me!" said the man. "I'll do anything. I promise!"

"All right," Norman said. "Tomorrow morning, when you're about to leave for work, turn back from the door and say casually to your mother-in-law, 'Mother So-and-so, how about having lunch with me today downtown, just the two of us?'"

The man stared at Norman as if he had lost his mind. "You must be joking," he said.

"Not at all," Norman replied. "And make it the best restaurant in town. Remember, you promised you'd do anything."

With many misgivings, but because he was a man of his word, the son-in-law took Norman's advice. To his amazement, when his mother-in-law appeared at the restaurant, she was a completely different woman, well-groomed, alert, intelligent, good-humored, a highly agreeable luncheon companion. Why? Because like all of us, she responded to attention, to being treated like a woman instead of like an undesirable piece of furniture. A completely new relationship was established, and it went on for many years.

The moral of the story—and this is probably the best single rule for anyone facing an in-law problem—is this: stop thinking of your marriage partner's relatives as a special breed known as in-laws (a term with faintly unpleasant connotations) and think of them simply as human beings with flaws and imperfections but also lovable qualities. Just discard the in-law label in your mind. Think of them as people. Treat them like people!

This was what I told the young wife who accosted me at church that Sunday. But I said some other things, too. "You tell me that your mother-in-law is full of energy and tends to take over. Instead of resenting this, why don't you turn it to your advantage? Which aspects of housekeeping do you dislike? Ironing? Sewing? Why not plan to have a small mountain of ironing on hand and ask your mother-in-law to do it for you? Do you need curtains made, or slipcovers? Get the material and leave it in her room. And while she does the work, get out of the house and do something with your husband. If she insists on taking over, let her take over tasks that you'd rather avoid anyway!"

I said another thing to the girl. "Instead of resenting your mother-in-law, why don't you make a study of her—a calm, thorough, objective analysis of what makes her tick? That's what I did with my mother-in-law. I tried to figure out what made her the way she was. I tried to understand her motives and her actions. In the process I learned an amazing amount about my husband and why *he* was the way he was. After all, Norman's mother had been the strongest influence in his life before I met him. Trying to understand her helped me to understand him.

"Finally," I continued, "you can turn this whole thing into a challenging exercise in controlling your own emotions. You're a member of this church; well, put your faith to work! Learn to forgive your mother-in-law for her intrusive or domineering ways. Remind yourself that she means well. Remember that if you're patient and kind with her, your husband will know it and appreciate it and love you all the more for it. Stop thinking about her visit as ten days of misery. Take it an hour at a time. Stop wringing your hands and stamping your foot and saying 'I can't stand it.' Tell yourself calmly that you can stand it and you will stand it and that you can even profit by it."

She thanked me and said soberly that I had given her some good and much-needed advice, and that she would try to do as I had said.

Before I leave this chapter, which seems to deal mainly with mothers-in-law, I might add a few words on the art of being one. It only takes one wedding ceremony to turn a mother into a mother-in-law, and this has happened three times in the last few years to me.

The basic rule, as everyone knows, is to be willing to

let go. To open that tight parental hand and set the child free, free to move surely and happily into a new life in which the parent can no longer be dominant. If it's your daughter who has married, you have to remember that she has a new identity, a new decision-making role. Don't give unsolicited advice, even when it seems to be needed. If you catch yourself doing it, as I admit I often have, bite your tongue and stop—in mid-sentence if necessary.

If your son has married, remind yourself that you no longer have a direct line into his life. A new situation exists, a triangle situation, which is much more complex. Look for something to praise in your daughter-in-law every time you're with her. If your son hears you speak well of the girl he has chosen, it makes him feel proud and happy, and strengthens the ties he still has with you.

When grandchildren start coming along, love them and admire them, but don't make suggestions about how they should be brought up. You may have your doubts, but it's better to keep them to yourself. I'm startled, myself, at the way *my* children seem to neglect *their* children's table manners. They seem to me to be extremely messy eaters. But theirs is a new generation, with new standards and new points of view. Who am I to say that I am right and they are wrong?

I'll make one firm point, though. If grandchildren are left in your house, then they are under your discipline and should conform to your standards. This can be a rude awakening for some youngsters, but there's no reason why an older person should be victimized in her own home by behavior which she does not wish to countenance.

A friend of mine had her two grandchildren for some days, a little girl of nine and her younger brother, age six. The boy was getting into everything and paying no attention to his grandmother's warnings. Finally she said, "Johnny, if you disobey me once more, I will not take you out for lunch with your sister and me. You will have to stay at home."

He understood, but paid no attention. At noon the grandmother took her little granddaughter and left the house amid screams from Johnny.

When she returned he came meekly to her and said, "Grandma, why didn't you give me a spanking like Mommy does and *then* take me out to lunch with you?"

Finally, I believe that a good-humored and fair-minded mother-in-law can be a great help to the people who marry her children by giving those people the benefit of her long experience in dealing with those children. All people have quirks and faults, and who knows them better than their own mother? Thus, I remember, I told Paul Everett, before he married our Margaret, that Maggie could be quite sharp-tongued and sarcastic at times . . . and he had better be prepared for this.

I told Lydia, who married our John, that she would have to get used to John's tendency to pounce on innocent words or phrases and try to read unintended meanings into them. I told John Allen, who married Elizabeth, that at times she could be hypersensitive and get her feelings hurt too easily, but that these reactions never lasted long. And I really think these little insights helped minimize potential areas of friction or misunderstanding in those marriages.

So . . . in-laws are not really outlaws; they're just plain, everyday people linked together in a relationship that is a bit more complicated and demanding than it would have been if somebody's daughter hadn't married somebody else's son.

The best formula for getting along inside that relationship? The same one that works in any relationship. It's called the Golden Rule.

10

THE INDISPENSABLE ART OF WIFELY PERSUASION

"Mrs. Peale," the young woman said, "I love my husband, but he's as hardheaded as a mule. He's the stubbornest man alive. When we disagree about something, it always has to be settled his way. When we argue, I never seem to get my point across. And I'm sick of it! Last night we had a knockdown, drag-out fight. Believe me, if we have many more like that, our marriage is going to wind up in the ash can!"

She was a pretty little thing with dark, expressive eyes that flashed as she remembered the events she was telling me about. I was in Boston for a meeting, a friend had kindly arranged a luncheon, and this young wife was seated next to me. She was a friendly, outgoing person. Evidently this problem with her husband was weighing on her mind, because she seemed anxious to tell me all about it. "He's a mule!" she repeated. "An ornery, balky, hammer-headed mule! One more row like that, and I'm going to walk right out of the house. I mean it, Mrs. Peale, I really mean it!"

"Well," I said mildly, "it's possible to have a disagreement without having a fight, you know. What were you disagreeing about?"

"Oh," she said disgustedly, "it was about our summer vacation. Paul is a great outdoorsman; he likes to go up to

Nova Scotia and fish and camp out. Well, that's all right. He works hard. He's starting his own advertising agency, and it's a struggle. He needs to get away for a while. But we went to Nova Scotia last summer. And the summer before that. This year I want to go down to my parents' place on Cape Cod. I love it there. It's where I spent the happiest days of my childhood. I know lots of people, and I can't help it if I prefer people to chipmunks and bears. My parents have a cottage on their place that we can have rent-free. It's cool and civilized and wonderful, and it's where I want to go!"

"Does your husband dislike Cape Cod?" I asked her.

"No," she said. "Not really. But he's one of these men who likes to keep on doing whatever he's *been* doing. He loves whatever is familiar. He hates to try anything new. And it's not fair! I thought about it all day yesterday, and the more I thought, the madder I became. So as soon as he got home from work, I let him have it. 'Paul Johnson,' I said to him, 'whether you like it or not, we're going to Cape Cod this summer. Not to Nova Scotia. And that's that!' "

"And how," I asked, "did he react to this—er—greeting?"

"He blew up. He said some awful things, and so did I. This morning was even worse, because he didn't say anything. Not a word. He just got up and drank some instant coffee and went to work." She looked at me and I could tell that this spirited, sophisticated young wife was miserable and frightened. "Oh, Mrs. Peale," she said, "what shall I do? Can you help me?"

"I think so," I said. "You're not the only woman in the world who's married to a stubborn man, you know. You're just going to have to try to master a subtle and tricky art, one that's an absolute *must* for any woman who wants her marriage to succeed. I had to learn it myself, the hard way. You can learn it too."

"What is it?" she demanded eagerly.

"Persuasion," I said. "The indispensable art of wifely persuasion."

I waited a moment for that to sink in. Then I continued: "Have you ever stopped to think how essential this thing called persuasion is, not only in marriage but in life? It's involved in just about everything that matters. You can't force anyone to be your friend. You can't make anyone love you or marry you. You can't compel anyone to hire you, or give you a raise. No matter how much authority you may have, you can't just bark orders and hope to get things done. There has to be a winning of acceptance, of agreement, of cooperation. There has to be successful persuasion—and there are certain rules for accomplishing this."

"Rules?" my luncheon companion repeated. "What rules?"

"The first rule," I said a bit drily, "is timing. Last night you broke that rule—smashed it into smithereens. Let's review the situation. Your husband comes home. You said he works hard, so we can assume he's tired. He's looking forward to a happy reunion with the woman he loves, a pleasant dinner, a restful evening. He opens the front door, and bang! As you put it, you let him have it. An ultimatum, on a touchy subject, before he's even had time to take off his hat! Now, an ultimatum is always a mistake, because it leaves everybody out on a limb with no way to climb down. But you weren't thinking about that. You were just thinking about yourself and what you wanted and how unfairly you've been treated. So you hurled your ultimatum. And your timing was terrible."

"Yes," she said slowly, "I guess it was."

"The second rule in the art of persuasion," I continued, "has to do with self-interest—the other fellow's. If you have a proposal, you've got to make him see what's in it for him. The other day in a speech my husband quoted something that Edmund Burke, the great English statesman, once said: 'What you make it the interest of men to do, that will they do.' I think that Mr. Burke was putting his finger on one of the great secrets of persuasion.

"But did you make a summer on Cape Cod seem like something that would be to your husband's advantage? You could have, you know. You might have pointed out, for instance, that he needs new clients for his advertising agency, that there are a lot more top executives on Cape Cod than there are in the wilds of Nova Scotia, and that he might easily meet some exceedingly valuable business contacts there. But you didn't do this. You merely shouted at him, 'We're going to Cape Cod because that's where *I* want to go!' Not a very compelling argument from where *he* sits. Am I right?"

"Yes," she murmured. "You're right."

"The third rule," I went on, "is this: Create a climate of acquiescence. It has become a joke, but there's a lot of insight in the old story about the little woman who fetches her husband's pipe and slippers, cooks him a splendid meal, tells him how young and handsome he looks and then asks him for a new car or a fur coat. I don't mean that you have to go in constantly for fulsome praise or insincere flattery. But if you're consistently thoughtful and considerate and just plain nice, your husband is going to love you that much more, and the more he loves you the more he'll be willing to give your wishes priority over his own—at least occasionally. Have you really been working at creating that sort of climate in your home? Or have you and your husband just been arguing about whose whims get preference, like two spoiled children quarreling over a lollipop?"

"I guess I could have worked harder at it," she admitted. She wrinkled her nose defiantly. "But so could Paul!"

I had to laugh. "I'm sure you both could! Now the fourth and last rule in this art of persuasion is patience. You can't always expect to have your hopes confirmed or your wishes granted instantly. You have to plant the seed of an idea, and then wait. If you insist on an immediate answer, very often it will be a negative one—because most people don't like to be backed into a corner."

"How can patience help me with this problem?" she wanted to know.

"Well," I said, "let me tell you about the time years ago when Norman and I were thinking of buying a house. We'd been married for thirteen years, but we'd never had one of our own. We'd always lived in city apartments. Now the children were growing up, and we wanted a place where we could see trees and grass and hills around us. We heard of an old farmhouse for sale on Quaker Hill in Pawling, New York, and we went to look at it.

"I fell in love with the house at first sight. It was an old eighteenth-century farmhouse set in about twenty acres of lovely rolling countryside. There was a wide lawn with great stately maples. There were original hinges on some of the doors, wide, hand-hewn floor boards, four fireplaces— with an old brick oven built into the largest one—and andirons that had supported blazing logs for more than 150 years . . . oh, all sorts of marvelous things!

"I was dying to buy that house, but Norman said flatly 'no' and gave all sorts of reasons. We didn't have the money. (This was true, but I knew we could borrow it.) The house was too big; we'd rattle around in it. (This was not so true; three children and some pets can fill up almost any house.) Finally, he said, the neighbor's barn cut off the view. (The barn did cut off some of the view, but not all—and anyway it was a gem of a barn: antique, picturesque, an impressive part of the landscape.)

"I tried to point out some of the features of the house that appealed to me, but Norman was not in a mood for listening. 'I'm sorry,' he said. 'We can't afford it, and I'm all against it, so you'd better forget about it.'

"I was tempted to argue, but I didn't. I didn't because I knew that the frugality built into Norman during his childhood was a very real and powerful thing. He was appalled by the prospect of going heavily into debt. I knew that summoning up the determination to break through that childhood conditioning would take time—and that nothing I could say would hurry the process. So I decided to wait—until the timing was right.

"While I waited, though, I applied the second rule of persuasion: self-interest. I didn't specify *what* place, but I reminded Norman from time to time that he needed a quiet, restful place to think, to write, to plan his speeches and sermons. I said I thought he would work better if he owned a piece of land somewhere. I remember I also got our friend, Lowell Thomas, for whom Norman has great respect and affection, and who also lives at Pawling, to tell him that the barn, with its hand-hewn beams, was one of the finest in the whole state of New York! Which it is.

"I also worked on creating a climate of acquiescence. In a lot of small things I made myself as agreeable and thoughtful as possible. I consciously put Norman's needs ahead of my own. And finally this paid off, because six months later, out of the blue, Norman suddenly said to me, 'Ruth, I know how much you loved that old farmhouse up in Pawling. I've been thinking. Maybe we could get a mortgage and somehow borrow the rest of the money . . .'"

Young Mrs. Johnson clapped her hands delightedly. "So you got it!"

"Yes," I said, "we got it. We had many happy years there. But you know, I'll confess something to you—my husband never was really reconciled to that barn. And so, almost a quarter of a century later, when another property came on the market not far away, with no barn and a really sensational view, I agreed to sell the house I loved and buy the one without a barn. Why? Because I had had my dream house for a long, long time. I thought it was high time my husband had his view!"

"And by doing that," she said thoughtfully, "you've created a new climate of acquiescence!"

"Well," I said, "I think we've got a kind of permanent one in our house by this time."

"I'm going right home," she said, "and start building one myself. I'll let you know how I make out!"

And she did, too. A few weeks later I got a telegram that said: "Two weeks in Nova Scotia, two on Cape Cod. Everything wonderful, thanks to you and the indispensable art."

She didn't even sign it.

She didn't have to!

❧ 11 ❧

HOW'S YOUR
APPRECIATION
CAPACITY?

❧ "If you want a man to keep loving you," my grandmother used to say, "you only have to do one thing —appreciate him, and let him know that you do."

That bit of homespun advice would save a lot of marriages, if more people put it into practice.

Just the other day, for example, an unhappy wife came to Norman, worried because love seemed to be draining out of her marriage. It wasn't that her husband was unfaithful, she said, or drank too much, or was stingy or jealous, or had any of the usual faults. It was just that he never praised her for anything she did, no matter how hard she tried. "It may be his ancestry," she said sadly. "His people came from Sweden. They're a rather stolid family; none of them is very good at expressing feelings. But I just can't go on like this. I feel as if something terribly important in me is drying up. If I can't get my husband to understand this, I may have to leave him."

Norman asked the husband to come and see him, and he did. Sure enough, he was a big, blond, blue-eyed man of Scandinavian parentage. When the situation was explained to him, he became rather defensive. "Why," he said, "this is all a lot of nonsense. I love my wife. She knows I love her. Why should I keep telling her so all the time?"

"This wife of yours," said Norman, "is she a good house-keeper?"

"Sure," said the man. "An excellent housekeeper."

"And a good cook?"

"Yes," said the man. "As a matter of fact, she's a terrific cook."

"When did you last tell her that?" Norman wanted to know.

"I don't remember," said this stubborn Swede. "But why should I tell her something she already knows?"

Now, Norman has a whole kit of psychological tools that he uses in his counseling work: stories, illustrations, quotations from philosophers and wise men, insights from the Bible, sometimes even jokes designed to make a point and hammer it into the listener's head. In this case, he reached into his kit and pulled out his William James illustration.

Norman rates William James, the great psychologist, as one of the finest minds America has ever produced. He told his visitor how James once wrote a book, a profound study of human nature, listing and analyzing all the emotions that motivate and control human behavior. The book was hailed as a masterpiece, but years later James was heard to say ruefully that he had neglected to include the most basic emotion of all. That emotion was the universal craving for recognition, the deep, unwavering desire in every human heart to be appreciated.

"Now tell me," said Norman to the big Swede, "what do you do for a living?"

His visitor said that he was a manufacturer of electrical appliances.

"Are they good appliances?" Norman wanted to know.

The Swede assured him that they were the best.

"Does it please you," Norman continued, "when your customers praise your product?"

The man admitted that it did.

"And is this praise a factor in making you want to keep up your standards and do your best?"

The man agreed that this was the case.

"Well," said Norman, "a woman who decorates a house, or cooks and serves a fine meal, or even irons a shirt skillfully is doing something just as creative as you are doing in manufacturing a good appliance. She needs and deserves praise and recognition just as much as you do. You may have a thousand customers, and so you have a thousand potential sources of appreciation. But she has only one—and that is you. Because you have failed to grasp this simple truth, your marriage is in danger. But fortunately there is a simple solution."

"What solution?" asked the man, now quite concerned.

"To begin with," said Norman, "when you go home from work this afternoon, take your wife some flowers."

"Flowers?" cried the Swede. "She'll think I'm suffering from a guilty conscience. She'll ask me what I've been up to!"

"Don't give her a chance to ask questions," Norman said. "Hand her the flowers and say, 'These are for you just because you are you!' "

The man finally agreed to carry out these instructions. The next day the wife called Norman and asked if he had prodded her husband into such unheard-of behavior. Norman just laughed and told her that he and her husband had had a talk, and that maybe this was the beginning of a new relationship. And from what we've heard since, it was.

Appreciation takes a thousand forms. It can be a casual compliment: "My, that's a pretty dress—or an effective hairdo—or a good-looking tie!" It can be an expression of deep affection and closeness: "Darling, I don't know what I'd do without you!" It can be a smile or a simple "Well done!" from a boss to a subordinate. We have a friend, a salesman, who has to travel a great deal. Whenever he goes on a trip, his wife writes a little note and hides it in his suitcase or in one of his pockets, just a line or two, telling him that she loves him, that she will miss him, that she thinks he's wonderful, that she knows the trip will be a success. I remember once he showed one of these notes to Norman and me. It said, "Why don't we make love twice as often?" Now there's a wife with a *real* sense of adventure!

There's no doubt about it: Appreciation in any form at any time brightens anyone's existence, however drab it may be. And like a beam of sunlight striking a mirror, the brightness is reflected right back at you.

One rule I've learned in my own efforts to master the art of appreciation is this: When the impulse comes to say the friendly thing, or do the little kindness that shows appreciation, act on it right away—otherwise it will vanish. Even when you realize how welcome a gesture of appreciation would be, it's terribly easy to put it off—and then forget all about it. I hate to think of the number of times I've thought of writing a note, or making a phone call, or sending a gift to express appreciation—and then failed to follow through. There's only one answer to this kind of procrastination: *Do it now!*

On a recent trip to Spain, for example, I needed a new evening dress so I ordered one made in Madrid. We were there only briefly, and the seamstresses in the couturier's salon worked overtime to have the dress ready. On the way to my last fitting, the thought crossed my mind that I really should do something to show my gratitude, something a little more tangible than mere verbal thanks. So I stopped the taxi, got out, found a store that sold candy, and bought some to take to the girls who had worked so hard on the dress.

You might have thought I'd brought them a bushel of emeralds! Nobody, apparently, had made such a gesture before. Their appreciation of my appreciation was so evident that I had a warm, good feeling all through my fitting and for the rest of the day.

It's really the old law of the echo in operation: When you send out an impulse of kindness or thoughtfulness, it comes bouncing right back to you. We have a friend, a housewife down in Florida, who always puts out coffee and doughnuts for the men who come to her back door to collect the garbage. She does it, she says, because she thinks they have just about the most thankless, disagreeable, and underpaid job in the whole structure of society. She went away on a vacation recently, and so the coffee breaks ended temporarily. But when she got back, all the garbage men climbed off their truck, came to the door, took off their gloves and solemnly shook her hand, asking about her trip and behaving like old friends. "We missed you," one of them said to her, "not because of the coffee, but because you really care about people!" She treasured that compliment as if it came from a prime minister—and she should have.

Every day every wife and husband should take a long, careful look at their married partner, decide what traits are most admirable, and seek out ways of expressing that admiration. In our marriage, for example, I try to appreciate how enormously difficult it is to create and deliver, week after week, year after year, sermons and speeches that will interest and inspire and help people. I remind myself how much effort and discipline—and sometimes discouragement —go into that kind of lonely task, a task that demands the very best that you've got to give, a task that no one else can ever do for you. I never cease to be amazed at the standards my husband sets for himself and the efforts he makes to live up to those standards.

I try to show my appreciation for this and for many other things by letting him know how much I admire his dedication, by praising him for his sermons or his speeches, by trying to shield him from unnecessary distractions and inter-ruptions and worries. Conversely, he is generous in telling me how helpful I am to him, how much he depends on me, how grateful he is for a home where things run smoothly and where his energies are not siphoned off into petty dis-tractions or details.

Not that we spend all our time doing this! Obviously, there's a line that divides sincere appreciation from over-effusiveness or calculated flattery. But I'm sure that for every person who oversteps the line, there are ten thousand who never even approach it.

That's why most of us need to make a conscious effort to be more appreciative of our marriage partners. Is your hus-band a commuter? Give some thought to the long, uncom-fortable hours he spends getting to and from his job. Take this into consideration when he gets home. Don't burden him with a lot of household problems the moment he steps off the bus or the train.

Does your wife have a job? Don't expect her to bring home a paycheck and also cope with all the housekeeping tasks by herself. Show your appreciation of her financial contribution by helping her with the dishes occasionally. You may be an executive in the office, but she's an executive in the home. A woman who runs a household, buying the groceries, cooking the meals, doing the laundry, coping with the children, making decisions about a thousand different details all day long, is just as much an executive as any businessman—maybe even more.

Simply showing interest in another person's activities can be a form of appreciation. It helps when someone asks: "How did your day go? What happened at the office? What did your women's club discuss this afternoon?" Routine questions? Certainly. And yet they make the other person feel that you're interested in what he does, that you want to share his burdens and his triumphs, that you care.

One family we know keeps their appreciation-level high with a sort of dinner-table game that they've worked out over the years. The father usually starts it by asking, "What was the most interesting thing that happened to you today?" (Or the funniest, or the most unexpected, or the most annoying—any superlative will do.) Then each member of the family responds in turn. Sometimes the father will ask, "What single thing in your life are you most grateful for right now?" The five-year-old may be grateful for her kitten. The ten-year-old may be grateful for his bicycle. The teen-ager may be grateful because his school's football team has won a game. The whole idea is to strengthen a sense of appreciation and encourage the expression of it.

Once, I remember, when we were visiting this particular family, we came down to breakfast on a bleak, rainy morning. "Well," said the father when we were all seated at the breakfast table, "this day looks a little dreary, I'll admit. But there must be some good things about it. Let's each try to name one good thing about this day."

So around the table they went. One of the children thought that the rain would make the farmers happy. Another said she liked the sound the raindrops made on the roof. A third said gravely that the day must be a good day because God had made it the way it was. The father said that it was a good day because they had good friends visiting them. Then it was the mother's turn. "It's a good day," she said, "because we're all together." She smiled at her husband. "But the best thing about this day, or any day," she said to him, "is you."

Appreciation . . . the best of all methods to use when you want to light a glow in somebody's heart, and feel the warmth of it in your own.

🌿 12 🌿

TOUGH QUESTIONS
FROM
TROUBLED SOULS

🌿 At a dinner party some years ago I found myself sitting next to a well-known novelist. During the evening someone complimented him on his ability to portray life exactly the way it is.

I remember how he smiled and shook his head. "That," he said to his admirer, "is exactly what I don't do. If I simply held up a mirror to life, nobody would be very interested, because anyone can observe what goes on around him. No, what a novelist tries to do is rearrange life. Life is the raw material. We reshape it so that it becomes more understandable and believable. Sometimes we give it a happy ending; sometimes not. In general, we try to portray life so that it makes a point—and that's what the craft of fiction is all about."

Often, as we have listened to people with deep personal problems, I have thought how wonderful it would be if, like the novelist, we could rearrange their lives and guarantee them happy endings. Quite often the raw material of real life can't be shaped so easily. It demonstrates the inescapable fact that the world is full of trouble and everyone will have his share sooner or later. But we point out the great fact that the world is also full of the overcoming of trouble. We emphasize that the twisted strands and tangled threads of people's lives *can* be straightened out, that trouble can be overcome, that life is really worth living in spite of the blows it deals. Sometimes we point out that partial solutions have to be accepted while one waits, with patience, for the final plan to unfold.

Still, this business of trying to help people with their problems remains one of the most fascinating and rewarding aspects of our lives. To give you some idea of the variety of the problems that are presented to us, and the varying insights we must employ in helping people, I have chosen a few recent situations out of the hundreds we have dealt with.

Here, then, are four scenes from this endlessly absorbing pageant, just as we witnessed them.

1. THE CASE OF THE REJECTED PARENTS

They sat close together on the sofa in our office, the husband's face lined with anxiety, the wife's eyes bright with unshed tears. Their story was a familiar one, too familiar. They had one child, a nineteen-year-old boy. He had started off well in college. Then his grades began to drop drastically. He complained that higher education was a waste of time, that his courses weren't relevant to modern life. He let his hair grow long and changed his style of dress from fairly conventional to very sloppy. He experimented with drugs, and did not try to hide this from anyone.

Finally he had written his parents a letter saying that he was going to drop out of college and roam around the country for a while, taking with him his guitar and a girl he had found who shared his ideas. The life his parents led, he said, was not for him; it was full of hypocrisy, it was indifferent to the suffering in the world and the misery of underprivileged people.

Their old-fashioned morality was antiquated and absurd. The government of the United States was imperialistic and warmongering. If the armed services wanted him, they would have to find him . . . and if they did, he would refuse induction even if it meant going to jail.

Greatly upset, the parents had gone at once to the college and tried to reason with the boy. They couldn't seem to reach him at all. They made every appeal they could think of; nothing made any impression. Finally he had taken his guitar and the girl—and the car his parents had given him for his nineteenth birthday—and had disappeared.

As the father told us this story, the mother twisted a handkerchief nervously in her lap. "How will they live?" she burst out when her husband finished speaking. "What will become of them? Where are they now? That's the worst part—not even knowing where they are!"

"When I see what they're doing to you," the husband said angrily to his wife, "I feel like breaking every bone in their stupid, selfish bodies. Here!" He thrust the letter his son had written toward us. "Look at this! No word of affection. No sense of gratitude for all we've done for him. No concern about what his behavior is doing to his mother. What's the matter with him? What's the matter with this whole younger generation?"

"We must have done something wrong," the wife said pathetically. "It must be our fault, somehow. But we just don't know what it is, or where we went wrong."

At this Norman spoke up sharply. "Don't feel so guilt-ridden. From what you tell us, the fault lies with your boy, not with you. Maybe you spoiled him a little, but not *that* much!"

I knew how Norman was feeling, because I was feeling the same way myself. These good people—and they *were* good people—had sought us out because they wanted to save their son, bring him back, restore him to the family circle like a prodigal son. But the ones who really needed help and support were the parents themselves. Why should their lives be ruined by the actions of one willful and selfish boy? The man still had his job, which was a good one. The woman still had her husband. They still had some good years to look forward to, if they didn't let this misfortune paralyze and embitter them.

So we said to them, "Look, this is a painful and deeply disappointing episode in your lives, but you are going to have to accept it, because you really have no choice. You can pray for your son. You can surround him in absentia with your love even if you don't know where he is. But there's nothing else you can do. You can't send the police after him and drag him home. It would do no good if you did. The boy has made it clear that he rejects the kind of life you have, the kind you had planned for him. He's nineteen years old, no longer a child. He's a person, a certain kind of person who has chosen a way of life radically different from your own. You have to let him go, in your minds and in your hearts. You can project prayers to him. And remember that unbelievable things happen through prayer. Your son may not even know what is influencing him.

"Then you must support and console each other. That is your big job now. You have your own lives to live, your own responsibilities and happiness to think about. So let him go!"

The father listened to us stoically, and I had the feeling that he was receptive to what we were saying. But the mother burst into tears. "It was something we did wrong," she insisted. "It must be our fault."

We tried to make her see that this was not necessarily the case. We told her that her son might easily have been swayed by influences that had nothing to do with his parents at all—a classmate with a strong personality and radical ideas, a teacher who for some reason took delight in attacking and undermining the values of his students. We told her that when young children are difficult or rebellious, the parent does have an obligation to keep working with them, trying to straighten them out, but that there has to be a cutoff point somewhere . . . and that once a youngster is in college he is old enough to think for himself and make his own choices.

"Remember this," Norman said, "you have just as much right to disapprove of his life-style as he does of yours. If trailing around the country with a guitar in one hand and an unwashed, unmarried girlfriend in the other is his idea of improving society, then you can't stop him. But you don't have to approve of it. And you certainly don't have to subsidize it."

"Don't worry," said the father grimly, "I won't."

"My dear," I said to the mother, "never stop hoping. Maybe he'll get tired of all this rebellion and defiance. Maybe after a few weeks on the road, home won't look so repulsive to him. Maybe he'll come back and bring some worthwhile ideas and experiences with him. Just put him in God's hands. And remember, you have to be ready for him if and when he does come back. Look at your life honestly. This is probably the greatest opportunity you will ever have to study yourself with utmost candor. Then try to change anything that needs changing within yourself. That won't be easy, but it is not impossible. And one thing is sure, it will be exciting."

"Yes," said Norman, "it might work out that way. Let's all have a prayer together that it will."

So we did . . . but how it all came out I cannot say, because we never saw them again.

2. THE CASE OF THE CHRONIC FAILURE

> The young man seemed unwilling to look Norman in the face. He sat with head bowed, shoulders slumped, the picture of dejection. Three days earlier, he said, he had lost his job. It was the third time this had happened to him in the past year. "I just don't seem to have what it takes," he kept saying. "Whatever I do always turns out wrong. Nothing I learned in school or college seems to apply to my basic problem, which is chronic failure. Aren't there any rules *anywhere* that can turn me around and point me toward doing things right?"

In telling me of this incident Norman admitted he had heard many such statements from discouraged people over the years. It suggests an agony of spirit that is very distressing indeed. But admitting to failure and asking for help are two very important steps in finding an answer to this problem. Although I cannot pretend to quote him verbatim, this is very close to what Norman said to his despondent visitor: "You're discouraged because you think you're a failure. The first thing you must understand is that right now you're a failure because you think you are. Thoughts are the most powerful things in the world. Yours are all downbeat and negative. Therefore everything you try to do turns out negatively.

"I can outline some rules for successful living, but you're the one who must apply them. Not just think about them. *Really apply them.*

"If you very much want something to happen in your life, here are five basic things you must do:

"First, have a goal. And not a fuzzy, but a sharply defined

goal. Moreover you must set a definite time limit within which you intend to achieve that goal.

"Next, pray about it. And the reason for praying is to be sure your goal is a right one, for if it isn't right, it's wrong, and nothing wrong ever turned out right. Check your objective with God, and see if it meets with His approval. In your case, if what you want is to be a confident, contributing member of society, I'm sure He does approve, and will help you if you ask Him for help.

"Third, picture yourself as reaching your goal, which may simply be succeeding in your next job. Concentrate every thought in your conscious mind on this objective. Banish all thoughts of failure.

"Fourth, let this image of yourself as succeeding sink deep into your unconscious mind, as it ultimately will if you persist in visualizing it. Once this happens, you will really have it, because it will have you.

"Fifth, face up to the fact that wishful thinking alone won't do it. You've got to make the necessary sacrifices. You've got to do the required work. You must never give in to discouragement. Never give up.

"If you can grasp these five principles," Norman told the young man, "and put them into action, at the very least you will cease being a failure and the chances are that you will become amazed at your ability to achieve successful results. I know this because I have seen so many people do it."

The young man asked a bit wistfully if he might hear about some examples.

"I could give you dozens," Norman said. "But let's settle for three. Take Roger Ferger, for instance, the now retired publisher of the Cincinnati *Enquirer*. I asked him, once, how he rose to such a prominent position in the newspaper world. He told me that as a boy, with no money and no particular goal in life, he happened to pass the newspaper building one day. Through a window he saw the editor working in his shirt-sleeves with a green eye-shade pulled down over his eyes. 'And suddenly,' Roger Ferger said, 'it seemed to me that to be able to reach people through the printed word, influence them, inform them, help them, was the most wonderful job in the world. At that very moment, right then, I decided not only that I was going to be a newspaperman, but that I was going to be publisher of the *Enquirer*. It was as definite as that. I never doubted that I could do it. I held the image in my mind and I worked until it came true!'

"That's one example," Norman told the young man. "Now here's another.

"At a Chinese dinner in Taipei, Taiwan, I met an old friend. Gladys Aylward was a diminutive lady. I noticed that, while seated, her feet didn't even touch the floor. She was dressed in Chinese costume, but she was British, quite British. Born in the Cockney section of London to a poor family, she worked as a maid in the home of a wealthy man.

"One day in London, she came upon a Salvation Army street meeting. Attracted by the music, she stopped and listened to the message of the speaker. For some reason she decided right then and there to become a missionary. But how could a poor, uneducated girl accomplish that objective?

"She began to read and continued until she became a sort of living encyclopedia on China. And then she felt the compulsion to become a missionary to China.

"She applied to the Mission Board, whose officials were highly intellectualized ecclesiastics. They gave this sincere girl an education test which she could not pass. 'You do not measure up to our standards; sorry, you can't go,' they said.

"But did that faze her? Not at all. She saved her money, shilling by shilling, and finally went out to China on her own. She began to speak in the streets of Nanking and Peking.

"This type of speaking went on week after week in many

Chinese cities. And it finally put her to the most dramatic test of her life.

"One day the governor of the province called her to his office and said, 'We have a terrible situation. There is a riot in the prison. Murderers and vicious men have overcome the guards and are running amuck. We can't go in; they will kill the guards if we try to enter. And one of the worst criminals in the prison has gone completely berserk. He is wielding a huge meat cleaver and has already killed two men and terrified everyone. I know you, for I have heard you speak. You have a God who gives all power. Please go in and disarm that man.'

"'You must be out of your mind, sir,' she said, aghast.

"'Oh, then you have not been telling the truth. I only know what I heard you say, and I believed you.'

"She realized then that if she ever wanted to speak again to the Chinese people she would have to go into that prison and demonstrate her belief.

"Gladys Aylward was admitted to the prison yard. The gate was quickly locked behind her. She saw the madman, the meat cleaver dripping with blood, chasing another prisoner.

"Suddenly, he was in front of her. He stopped short, amazed. They stood facing one another—the little woman and the incensed giant.

"She looked into his wild and feverish eyes, then calmly said, 'Give me that weapon.' He hesitated for a moment, and then meekly handed the meat cleaver to her.

"She told the prisoners she would plead for clemency if they would surrender. And they did. Later, she received a just settlement of their grievances with the governor.

"Your problems, or mine, of course, may never be as dramatic as the one Gladys Aylward had to handle. But there is a power in everybody that can be summoned up in a crisis.

"Her life was so unusual that it became the story for a

full-length Hollywood movie with top stars clamoring for the privilege of playing her part. It was called *The Inn of the Sixth Happiness*. She never let go of her dream.

"The third story I'd like you to consider," Norman went on, "involved a sickly child from the back streets of a great city who was sent to stay with an old aunt who lived in the country. It was thought that the fresh air and simple life on the little farm might restore the child to health.

"One day, after she had been there for a while, her aunt told her to go down to the spring at the foot of the hill. There she would find a large, rectangular stone. She was to bring this stone up to the farmyard and put it by the kitchen door.

"When the child saw the size of the stone, she came back and told her aunt that such a task was beyond her. She couldn't possibly carry the stone up the hill. She couldn't even lift it. The aunt replied calmly that she could bring it up, and she would, even if she only succeeded in moving it a few inches a day.

"For weeks the child struggled with the stone, pushing it, shoving it, dragging it inch by inch, foot by foot, up the hill. Finally, exhausted but triumphant, she got it to the kitchen door. Only then did she ask her aunt why she wanted it there. 'I don't care about the stone,' the old woman said with a smile. 'I just wanted to teach you a lesson—that there's *nothing* you can't do, if you make up your mind to do it, and never quit!'

"And," concluded Norman, "Althea Gibson did learn that lesson, because she overcame her health problems and went on to become the first black woman tennis champion the game has ever known."

The young man had been listening with growing hope and resolve in his eyes. "Maybe you're right," he said. "Maybe I can lick this thing. If those people could do it, maybe I can too."

"You *will* do it," Norman promised him, "if you just change your mental attitude. Remember now, it can't be a superficial change. It has to be a change in depth. In a way, it's vertical thinking. When you do it right, the thoughts rise up to God and then come back to you, and the power flows along this vertical line. Try it. You'll see."

"I will," said the young man. "I really will."

"And," said Norman to me, "from the set of his shoulders as he went out the door, I believe he really did."

3. THE CASE OF THE MISGUIDED MOTHER

I knew the couple quite well—modern, well-educated, intelligent people with a couple of reasonably well-adjusted teen-agers in high school. So far as we knew, they were a happy, congenial family. I was surprised, then, to get a telephone call one day from the wife, whose name was Betty.

"Ruth," she said, "I wonder if Don and I could come and talk to you and Norman. We don't agree about something. In fact, we've quarreled rather badly. We need some straight thinking, and I believe you could help. I guess we want you to tell us who's wrong and who's right."

So they came to our office conference room and told their story, a curious one, but all too typical of the troubled times in which we live. It seemed that their sixteen-year-old daughter Linda had come home from school with a couple of "joints"—marijuana cigarets. She showed them quite casually to her mother. "Now don't get up-tight, Mom," she said. "Everyone smokes a little pot now and then. It's a lot less dangerous than the alcohol your generation seems to prefer. It's not habit-forming, either. Why don't you try it with me, just for fun? It can't hurt you. And it'd do a lot more to bridge the generation gap than ranting and raving the way most parents do."

All this occurred in the late afternoon before Betty's husband came home from work. She hesitated, then made a spur-of-the-moment decision. She sat down on the floor of her daughter's bedroom and took a few drags of the "joint." Aside from a stinging sensation in the back of her throat, she felt no effects at all, and went back to her housework.

When her husband came home, Betty told him what she had done—and he hit the ceiling. Betty, unsure of herself and highly defensive, reacted with anger. A grim family quarrel had ensued, and it was still unresolved.

"I don't approve of drugs any more than Don does," Betty said. "But I believe good communication with your children is more important than a couple of puffs of smoke. Linda was being honest when she showed me those two miserable cigarets; she could have concealed them and smoked them in secret quite easily. In a way I think she was testing me, to see if I was on her side. I believe that by putting aside my own scruples and refusing to act conventionally I strengthened the bond between her and me. She considers me her friend as well as her mother, and believe me that's pretty rare nowadays!"

Don took a completely opposite view. "It was a terrible mistake," he said. "I know that they are investigating the dangers and effects of marijuana, but smoking it is still against the law. And when a parent breaks a law he becomes a lawbreaker. What's worse, in this case, the parent was aiding and abetting a teen-ager in breaking the law. I think that what Betty did was immoral and wrong—and I suspect that she thinks so too, although she won't admit it."

In this case, without hesitation, we sided with the husband. "I can understand the motives that led you to handle the situation as you did," I said to Betty. "Every mother wants to feel close to her children, wants to be accepted by them. And maybe there was a momentary conspiratorial lets-all-be-daring-together feeling. But I'm sure you lost more than you gained. Your daughter needs to live within a framework of rules, and she wants her parents to enforce those rules even though she may rebel against them sometimes. If a parent joins in the rule-breaking, the children become confused, perhaps even resentful. Certainly they lose respect for the parent who gets down on their level in a situation like this."

"That makes sense to me," Norman said. "And there's always the danger that their reaction may be, 'Well, Mother didn't object to my smoking pot, so why should I think twice about trying something a little stronger, like heroin, or amphetamines, or even LSD?' There may be no proof that using marijuana inevitably leads to experimentation with more dangerous drugs, but certainly there is a psychological connection. Most drug addicts admit that marijuana was the first step, and that's the step you were actually taking with your daughter."

At this point Betty began to weep. "All right," she said. "I was wrong. I can see that now. In fact I knew it at the time but we parents have been put in the position of having to do anything to avoid the ill will of our children. But the harm is done, I guess. What can I do about it now?"

"If I were you," Norman said, "I'd call a family conference and go over the whole thing, honestly and candidly. Admit you made a mistake. Try to explain why. Make your daughter see that your intentions were good, but misguided. Stress all the points we've been making here. If you and Don do an honest, effective job, and do it together, I predict you'll come out of the conference with more respect from your children and more real closeness than you've ever had before."

Don put his arm around his wife. "We'll do it!" he said. And they did. And it worked, for later the daughter said that right in the middle of the family conference a sudden resolve swept over her and she never touched pot, or any other drug, from that moment on.

4. THE CASE OF THE UNHAPPY WIDOW

She was a pretty woman in her mid-thirties, quietly dressed, with ash-blonde hair and unhappy, dark brown eyes. She told me, with a faint smile of resignation, that she didn't think I could help her with her trouble. But she had asked for an interview, anyway. Her problem turned out to be poignantly simple. She loved her husband—and he was dead.

He had been dead, it seemed, for over a year. A sudden heart attack had killed him, without warning. After the first grief and shock were over, his widow went back to her job as a receptionist in a doctor's office. She had tried desperately, she said, to make some sort of adjustment, to achieve some sort of acceptance. But her life was one long ache of loneliness.

The woman and her husband had had no children, which had drawn them even closer together. She had a mother and a sister, but they lived in a distant city. She had the usual quota of friends—all of whom were kind, but who also, she said resignedly, tended to forget a widow when it came to making plans for parties or get-togethers.

I asked if she had gone out at all with other men since her husband's death.

Yes, she told me, a few times. But it was difficult. Most men apparently thought that a widow would be sex-starved and available. "I may be sex-starved," she said wryly. "In fact, I know I am. But I'm not available. You see, I happen to have some standards. I'm still in love with Jim. That rules out any other man for me."

"Tell me," I said to her, "do you think remarriage is a possibility for you some day?"

"I suppose so," she replied. "But I don't think much of widows who rush around trying to catch a man whether they're in love with him or not."

"Of course," I said slowly, "but perhaps you're being a little too defensive about all this. Perhaps unconsciously you feel that your late husband wouldn't want you to remarry."

She made a little gesture of helplessness. "It's not really remarriage that I worry about. It's this lost feeling, this terrible emptiness. It's as if part of me had been cut away."

"That's understandable," I said. "A part of you *has* been cut away, temporarily, at least."

She put her clenched fists suddenly up to her temples. "I hate it," she said in a choked voice. "I hate being alone. I hate being a widow!"

"Why don't you stop applying that word to yourself? It's loaded with all sorts of gloomy connotations. When you keep calling yourself a widow, you're almost labeling yourself a has-been. Why not think of yourself as a single, unmarried person, with the emphasis on that last word. You're still a *person*, with all the unique qualities that made your husband love you and your friends admire you. If you're working in a doctor's office, you're still serving a very useful function. You're helping people. You're pulling your weight in the boat."

"The daytime hours aren't so bad," she said. "It's going home alone and knowing no one is there. It's so different from what . . . from what . . ." She couldn't go on.

"I know," I said, full of pity for her. "I know because I've heard that from other women who have lost their husbands.

The hours between five P.M. and seven P.M. are somehow the worst."

"Tell me, Mrs. Peale," she said, "what would you do if suddenly you found yourself in my shoes—and I hope you never do."

"Well," I said, "I think I would tell myself that some loneliness was inevitable, and just tighten my belt and try to hold on. I'd be as natural and normal as I possibly could. I'd look for new interests. I might take up some special project that would force me to get out of the house and make contact with other people. For example, I might ask the Federation of Women's Clubs if they could use me as a speaker. I'd entertain a great deal more than I do now, and I'd try to include people who are lonely. Above all I'd keep telling myself that the separation from the person I love most was only temporary . . . that some day, as the Bible promises, I would see him again."

She nodded slowly. "Yes," she said, "I try to remember that promise."

"There's only one answer to your problem right now," I told her gently. "You have to make up your mind not to give in to grief or to loneliness. You must keep going. You also have to face up to the fact that sometimes, if it's prolonged beyond a certain point, grief can be a self-centered thing. Let me tell you about a lady Norman met one day in the lobby of the Commodore Hotel.

"He was going to a Rotary luncheon, and saw this woman sitting forlornly in the hotel lobby. He recognized her as the wife of a former Rotarian who had died a few months before. He approached her and asked what she was doing there. She told him, with tears, that ever since her husband's death she had come to the hotel every Thursday when the Rotary Club met. She would sit in the lobby and think about her husband and shed a few tears and finally go home.

"Norman asked her to wait until the luncheon was over,

and she did. He then spoke to her kindly but bluntly. He told her that what she was doing was morbid and depressing, and that her husband—who had been a jovial, outgoing man—would be the first to disapprove. He asked her what she was doing with herself aside from sitting around grieving. When she admitted that she was doing little or nothing, he took her down to the Marble Church where a group of volunteers was busy mailing out booklets of inspirational material. 'Put this lady to work,' he said to the volunteer-in-charge, 'and when she's done whatever you give her to do, think of something else to keep her busy!' In the end, he helped the woman find a permanent position as an unpaid volunteer in a large charitable organization, and gradually—thinking about others instead of herself—she was able to find peace of mind and a degree of contentment.

"What she did," I said to our visitor, "you can do too. Don't brood about the past or worry about the future. Time is on your side, because it does heal wounds and bring new opportunities for living. You're still young, you're still attractive; I feel sure that God has great plans for your life, if you'll just trust Him and be patient."

Our unhappy visitor was looking very thoughtful. "I'll try," she said. "Thank you for everything." She gave me a wonderful smile, and was gone.

So it goes, year after year. People with difficulties; people with sorrows; people with problems. Almost all of them lovable, appealing human beings. Sometimes we can help. Sometimes not. But we put them all in God's hands. And the challenge never grows stale. To serve God by trying to serve people lies at the heart of all true happiness—and of the adventure of being a wife.

✳ 13 ✳

HOW TO
BE
HAPPY

✳ Quite often, after I have given a talk to some church group or women's club, there is a question-and-answer period in which anyone can bring up anything that's on her mind. The other day a young woman in her late twenties or early thirties stood up and fired a direct and uncompromising question. "Mrs. Peale," she said, "are you a happy person?"

Fortunately, I didn't have to hesitate. "Yes," I said, "I am."

"Well," she said, "how do you do it? What makes you that way? I'm not a really happy person. Oh, I pretend to be most of the time. But this thing called happiness eludes me. I think it eludes most of my friends, too, although some will deny it. I know very few happy people, if any. There are just too many problems and tensions and frustrations in the average person's life these days. So if you are happy, I wish you'd tell us how you got that way, and how you stay that way, and how we can be happy too."

The audience grew very quiet and expectant, the way an audience does when a topic deeply interests people. I drew a deep breath, said a quick silent prayer and then talked for five or six minutes. To the best of my recollection, what I said went something like this:

I can't offer you any absolutely foolproof formula for happiness. I doubt if anyone can. But I can tell you a few things that I have found out about it, things that have been useful to me.

First of all, I'd advise you to stop struggling to be happy. Happiness isn't something that you can deliberately set out to achieve for yourself, like skill at typing or a college degree. In fact, the more you focus on your own happiness, or lack of it, the more it will continue to elude you. This is because preoccupation with self seems to be the enemy of happiness. The more concerned you are with your own pleasures and successes—or your own problems and failures, for that matter—the less contented you are going to be.

As wiser people than I have pointed out for centuries, the best way to get happiness is to give it. I've heard my husband quote Emerson—something to the effect that it's impossible to sprinkle perfume on another person without having some of it come wafting back to you. I don't know why more women who are idle and restless and basically bored don't grasp this fundamental fact. Playing bridge or playing golf is fine—as a diversion. But in terms of deep-down happiness that sort of activity can't begin to compare with volunteer work in a hospital, or leading a Girl Scout troop, or helping underprivileged people in some direct and personal way. How many such outlets do you have in your life right now? If you'll double them, you'll be quadrupling your chance for this thing called happiness.

And it may sound strange, but I have found that solving problems, really solving them, can give a good, happy feeling. We all have the problems and tensions and frustrations of everyday living; no one is immune. But there are useful techniques for dealing with problems, and ways of minimizing tensions. For instance, in my husband's life there are dozens of problems to be faced, endless writing deadlines to be met, scores of administrative details to handle. I found out long ago that Norman is brilliantly capable of dealing with these successfully so long as they come at him one at a time. If they're all dumped in his lap at once, if they all come clamoring for attention together, he gets harassed and irritable—as well he might.

So I give myself the task of shielding him from the avalanche as much as I possibly can, of seeing to it that the problems are presented one at a time so that he can really concentrate on each one and dispose of it before the next one comes along. That way, he works along smoothly and efficiently and happily.

In my own case, too, when I'm faced by some big, ugly, complicated problem, instead of just staring at it in gloom and despair, I've learned to make myself analyze it, break it down into less formidable fragments, fragments that I can tackle right away with some hope of success. I've found that if you chip away at a problem, piece by piece, you can often whittle it down to a size you can manage. And getting a problem under control will add to anyone's happiness.

This was dramatized for me years ago up at our farm when one of our maples died. We were afraid that if a strong wind came up, it might fall against the house and damage it. So we had to have the tree taken down.

Norman and I thought that the tree expert would just saw through the trunk and let the whole thing crash to the ground. But he didn't do it that way at all. First he trimmed off the small upper branches. Then, one by one, he sawed through the great limbs and lowered them with ropes and pulleys. Then he began taking down sections of the huge trunk, piece by piece, until there was only about twenty feet left. Finally he sawed this down, and the whole tree was gone. "We always tackle the easy part first," he said. "That way, the rest of the problem gets simpler and simpler as we go along." Norman was so impressed that he used the story as an illustration on problem-solving in one of his sermons. And I've been using it myself with good results ever since.

I think, also, I'm a genuinely happy person because I am fortunate in being really quite free from disturbing inner conflicts. Norman says I'm well-organized. The fears and anxieties that seem to bother so many people are no problem to me. And for this I'm very thankful, having observed what fear does to some.

We all have problems, and there's no doubt that problem-solving may remove specific causes of unhappiness. But this alone won't provide the peace of mind, the quiet sense of joy and fulfillment that I think you're talking about. This is a gift that life bestows when you live a certain way and observe certain rules. Religion has always known this, and the Bible has a great deal to say about it. That's why some of the happiest people I know are those who have a strong religious faith—and some of the unhappiest are those who have none. After all, if you believe that the Power that runs the universe loves you, is concerned about you, cares for you and will help you, how can you be anything but happy, no matter what difficulties you may be facing?

Long ago I put my life in God's hands and I simply trust Him: trust His love; trust His watchful care. Because I've always tried to grow spiritually, I believe I have no resentments. I don't hate anybody and I try to take my disappointments graciously. If a plan doesn't work out I simply ascribe it to God's guidance and ask what He desires to teach me. Now, don't get the idea that I'm perfect. Ask Norman. He will tell you.

I'll give you one example of the kind of happiness that comes through faith. Some years ago my husband was speaking at a convention of businessmen in Chicago. It was in the ballroom of one of the big hotels, and I noticed that as he spoke some of the waitresses who had served us were standing along the wall listening. We had a plane to catch right after the talk. We had said our good-byes and were walking through the lobby when we heard someone calling our name. We turned and saw one of the waitresses in her uniform hurrying after us. She had one of the sweetest, happiest faces I ever saw on anybody. She rushed up to Norman and cried, "Oh, Dr. Peale, I just love you!"

"Well," laughed Norman, "I love you too. But what has happened to make us love each other so much?"

"I'll tell you," she answered. "I have a little boy. His father deserted us soon after he was born, but I thanked God all the more that He'd given me this wonderful baby boy. Then when my boy was five years old, he got sick. The doctor told me it was very serious. He said, 'Mary, you've got to be strong. I don't know whether we can save your boy or not.' He was preparing me for the worst. I was in despair. I felt that my whole world would collapse if I lost my boy. He was all I had, and I loved him so.

"Then a neighbor gave me one of your sermons to read. In it you said, 'If you have a loved one who is ill or about whom you are worried, don't hold this loved one too closely. Surrender him to God. God gave him to you. He isn't yours, really, he is God's. So give him to God, for God is good. He's a great, kind, loving Father who holds each of His children in His love.'

"Well," she continued, "I'd never heard anything like that before. And it seemed awfully hard to do, but something inside me told me that it was right. So I prayed the way you said, and put my boy in God's keeping." And she held out her hands as if she were lifting up a child into the great arms of God.

"And what happened?" Norman gently asked.

Smiling through tears of joy, she said, "Isn't God good! He let me keep my boy. And now God and I are raising him together."

A number of other waitresses, Mary's friends, had joined us and stood listening. There were tears in everybody's eyes, including mine. I guess there are always tears when you come into the presence of that kind of happiness.

You can't demand it. You can't buy it. You can't even earn it. It's a gift. But you have to want it. You have to accept it. You have to reach out for it. If I were you, that's what I'd do.

14

YOUR CHILD'S HAPPINESS IS YOUR OWN

One of the greatest satisfactions a parent can have is the feeling that some of the good things, the good impulses, the good insights that you have tried to teach your children have taken root and grown into strong, healthy character-traits. After I had given that little talk on happiness to the members of that women's club, I wished I had stressed this point. But that's the trouble with speeches: You always remember what you really wanted to say after you sit down.

Still, the nice thing about writing a book is that you can always start another chapter and correct the omission. So that's what I'd like to do now, and I'd like to let my older daughter Margaret speak for herself. I think you'll agree that she speaks very well, and that the story she tells is worth listening to. I know that as her mother I feel a deep glow of pride when I read this story of Maggie's. In a way, it's the story of the moment in which she ceased to be a child and became a woman and a wife in the deepest sense of both words.

A few years after Margaret and her husband Paul Everett were married they sadly came to acceptance of the fact that they were not to have any children of their own. This, of course, was a great blow. Margaret was deeply unhappy about it. She was always one to keep her feelings to herself, but finally she consented to tell her story of adopting a baby girl. (Later Paul and Margaret also adopted a baby boy, and both are wonderful children.) In this poignant story written for *Guideposts* magazine, her own secret of happiness comes through. As I said above, a victory by one of your own children deepens your own happiness. Here is Margaret's story:

What was I so nervous about? This was the moment I had waited for, prayed for. It was ten A.M., and I was to look at our new baby for the first time.

"How do you feel?" Miss Nelson, our caseworker, asked as we sat in the waiting room of the adoption agency.

"I didn't sleep a wink last night," I replied. "And at this moment I could turn around and walk right out of here."

Miss Nelson laughed. "Believe me, you aren't the first prospective mother to feel that way. But it won't be long. I'm on my way to get the baby now."

As she left the room I sank back into the couch. I knew what was wrong with me, that my panic was more than nervous excitement. I turned toward my husband, Paul, in a desperate effort to calm myself and whispered my secret fear.

"What if I don't like the baby!"

Paul reminded me that almost a year before we had prayed earnestly about our decision to adopt, in the belief that if we were open about ourselves, God would use His instrument—the agency—to place the right baby with us.

In our first adoption interview months before, Miss Nelson had emphasized that there were no right or wrong ways to feel about children. "The important thing is for you to understand and express how you really feel, not how you think you should feel," she had said.

This startled me because somehow I had felt that certain attitudes toward children were expected of adoptive parents. Because I couldn't have my own, I should love all children, when the truth was I wanted a healthy baby of a background similar to ours—not just any child who needed a home. I finally told this to Miss Nelson, somewhat apologetically, but also to test her attitude. Could I really tell her how I felt?

"That's fine," she said. "You want a child you could have produced yourself. I don't blame you."

I also told her my shock and self-pity when I couldn't get pregnant. I confessed that I didn't want a baby with a handicap, even a correctable one. "I guess I really want a perfect baby," I stammered hesitantly.

I had been as honest as I knew how to be about my feelings. Then some months later we were approved. Yet a tiny fear, lodged in the back of my brain, kept asserting itself. What if I didn't like the baby they chose? I would be drawn naturally to a cute infant, but what if I wasn't drawn to the one the agency gave me?

Every instinct told me that a mother instantly loves her baby. Hadn't I seen pictures and read stories of adoring mothers looking down into the faces of their scrawny, wrinkled, red little babies? And I, as a new mother in a different way, would *have* to feel that same outpouring of love or question my motherhood.

I turned from the window in the waiting room as I heard the elevator clang open. A little cry echoed down the hall, and my heart thudded into my stomach. No, please, not yet—but before I could finish the sentence, Miss Nelson stood in the doorway cradling a bundle.

She came toward me, and I had to look at the tiny face peeking through the blanket. She was very little— five weeks old, eight and a half pounds—very scrawny and pale. I took her and smiled at Miss Nelson. I smiled because I had to, not because I wanted to. I didn't exactly feel like crying. I just didn't feel anything.

When Miss Nelson departed, leaving the three of us alone, my husband and I made cooing and clucking noises to the baby and light conversation with each other. "She's got a beautifully shaped head," Paul said. "And lovely blue eyes." Yes, I thought, but she isn't blonde and she isn't cute.

Miss Nelson returned, and I drifted through the formalities and thank-you's. The elevator clanged again and carried us to the street and our new life.

Jennifer's first few weeks at home were a nightmare. She cried constantly and slept little. I walked around in a daze, wondering where all my peace had gone and why I had wanted a baby in the first place. I had expected the usual demands, but not such a total involvement of time as now faced me. People came and went. Night and day followed in sequence, and I followed automatically.

I put on the happy new-mother face valiantly, especially to Miss Nelson who called several times, but I was never far from tears. I didn't feel anything for this baby and I was terrified. I was sure that my anxiety had a lot to do with Jennifer's behavior, yet it became a vicious circle. The only thing that kept me going was my husband's *certainty* that this was our baby.

I watched Jennifer grow those next few weeks.

Amazingly, our best times were the two A.M. feedings. The hour was so still and Jennifer was playful and relaxed. So was I. Six o'clock was too close to the beginning of a new day, and at ten P.M. my equanimity was at the breaking point. But at two A.M. we enjoyed each other, and I began to feel her warmth, spontaneity, and alertness. I was delighted at how perfectly her body was formed and I counted over and over again her ten tiny fingers and ten toes.

When Jennifer was two months old we went to the doctor for a routine checkup. At the end of the examination he said, "I think you should take her to see an orthopedist. Her feet are pointing out rather strangely, and he might want her to wear braces for a while."

As the day of our appointment with the orthopedist approached, I told myself a hundred times not to worry, that the doctor was only being cautious. But as we got into the car all my fears bubbled to the surface. Braces! What if something terrible is wrong? What if she'll never walk!

All of a sudden, as I thought about the possibilities of tragedy for my baby, something happened to me. The thought burst into my mind, like the spring flower that finally pokes its head above the ground: I love this baby. I love this precious little person beside me. I love the smile which comes more frequently now, the tiny hands that reach eagerly for me, the wispy brown hair that glistens in the light. I love her blue eyes that take in the world and seem to analyze everything before bestowing approval.

Tears were streaming down my cheeks. She is my baby, and I love her. She is God's gift to me, and I'm not going to let anything happen to her. Suddenly I knew that God had taught me a great lesson about love. It isn't giving birth that makes you love a baby—

or, in my case, instant attraction—but taking care of him and sharing in his growth.

I pulled into the doctor's parking lot and switched off the engine. I lifted Jennifer out of the infant seat and held her. "Do you know Mommy loves you?" I said, leaning toward her. I imagined I saw a nod, but I know I saw a smile light up her face and eyes.

She was beautiful.

✻ 15 ✻

THE HEALING
ART OF
ABSORPTION

✻ Sometimes I think the best epitaph a wife could hope for would be just six words: "She was a wonderful shock absorber." Carved on a headstone, that might not look very elegant or very spiritual, I know. But to go through life cushioning shocks or blows for other people calls for a set of characteristics very close to the Christian ideal. It calls for selflessness, service, compassion, kindness . . . just as religion does.

Being a shock absorber comes easily to a mother, because it's reinforced by instinct. Your toddler falls and bangs his forehead; your second-grader burns his fingers on a hot stove; your teen-ager is in tears because her feelings have been hurt by some thoughtless friend. Here the protective instinct is swift and sure: you dry the tears, you say the consoling or comforting thing, you put the right medicine—physically or emotionally—on the hurt. In a way, you are protecting and restoring yourself, because your child is a part of you.

But it's more difficult for husbands and wives to respond so automatically to each other's needs. Here two adults are involved, two separate and sometimes demanding egos. In dozens of marriage situations, affection whispers: "This is my man (or woman): I love him; therefore I will try to spare him and protect him." But there is also a contrary voice, a churlish sort of voice that grumbles: "Well, he's a grown man, isn't he? He ought to be able to cope with his own problems. Besides, I've got my own difficulties . . . and what's he doing to help me?"

In other words, where marriage is concerned, no one is a natural, ready-made shock absorber. It's an art—and you have to learn it, just the way you learn any other skill or art.

What does it take to learn it? It takes intelligence, discipline, practice at anticipating trouble, adroitness at moving to head it off or minimize it. Above all, it takes motivation. You have to be able to see clearly that the more you can spare or shield your marriage partner, the stronger and deeper will be his gratitude and his affection for you. Let's face it. We're all human. We're going to love and appreciate those who make our lives happier and easier, not those who do the reverse.

It doesn't matter whether your husband is a bus driver or the President of the United States, there are always ways in which a wife can ease the burden, reduce the tension, eliminate unnecessary worry. I have known Pat Nixon for years, and I have watched her master the art. Long before her husband entered the White House, she had trained herself to be an ideal wife for a man in the heat and battle of politics: always loyal, always available, always supportive. Never putting herself or her needs ahead of his. Never complaining about separations or long-working hours. Her courage and composure in the face of that howling mob in Latin America were tremendous.

Her self-control is just as admirable. I remember her face on television the night her husband lost the election to John F. Kennedy by a paper-thin margin. I remember the tears in her eyes as she held her head high and tried to smile. I never admired a woman more. She certainly helped to earn the triumph that finally came to her husband.

So much for the wife of the President of the United States. As for the wife of a bus driver . . . well, I know one who is just as supportive. Fred and Betty are strong Christians, good citizens, the salt of the earth, and dear friends of ours. Fred is a New York City bus driver. He is a sensitive, high-strung person. But he didn't always think highly of himself; in fact, he thought he was a failure. He looked upon bus driving as an unimportant task. But he had been at it for so long that changing jobs would have been difficult. He wasn't really trained for anything else.

This sense of personal inadequacy kept gnawing away at Fred until one day his wife could stand it no longer. She sought out Norman and me and asked, "What on earth can I do to bring happiness into Fred's mind? What can I do to make him feel that his job is important? I'm convinced that it is. He helps people who ride in his bus by being cheerful and patient and friendly. He watches old ladies and young children to see that they don't get into trouble. But still he feels inferior. Do you think you could possibly talk to him? He doesn't really listen to me."

We said we would, and Norman did talk to Fred. "I tried," he told us later, "to make him see that if you're serving people—which he is—you're serving God. And if you're serving God, one form of service is as honorable and worthwhile as another."

"Did you get through to him?" I asked.

Norman shook his head doubtfully. "I don't know. He agreed with everything I said. But I had the feeling that he was just being polite. I also had the feeling that until Fred is able to straighten up and look people in the eye with pride and confidence and *say* he's a bus driver, he'll never be at peace with himself."

"I'm afraid you're right," I said.

Now, Fred was an expert driver of any kind of car, and quite often he would offer to drive us to a dinner or a speaking engagement out of town. This suited us fine, because Norman never liked to drive when he had a speech on his mind, and I found it easier and pleasanter to relax with him instead of battling with the traffic myself. On these expeditions, Betty usually joined us, and the four of us always had a fine time riding out and riding back.

One rainy night Fred and Betty drove us out to a country club in New Jersey where Norman was to be the after-dinner speaker. It was quite an elaborate affair, with important men and women from all over the state—politicians, business tycoons, high-ranking military people, and so on. Fred and Betty had planned to go to a restaurant for dinner, and then come back for us. But on this occasion, at the last minute, two guests were unable to come, and Norman asked the host if the two friends who had driven us out from the city could take their places.

The host was very gracious and said he'd be delighted. But Fred hesitated. When we kept urging him, he mumbled, "I'm just a bus driver. I don't belong with those people in there."

Then up spoke Betty, lovingly but firmly. "Fred," she said, "you're my husband, and I love you, and I'm proud of you, and as long as I feel that way I don't see any reason in the world why we shouldn't accept these good people's invitation."

Fred looked at her for about half a minute without a word. "All right," he said finally, "if that's the way you feel, we'll do it."

They took the two seats, not far from us, and everything seemed to be going fine until suddenly, in one of those unexpected lulls that always seem to happen at dinner parties, I heard the man across the table from Fred—he was an international banker, a very prominent man—say, "And what line of business are you in, sir?"

I held my breath, because the whole table seemed to be

listening, and I knew Betty was holding hers, too. Then all of a sudden Fred smiled, a friendly, relaxed smile. "I drive a bus," he said. He said it loud and clear, but the banker was so taken aback that he evidently thought he hadn't heard Fred correctly. "You do *what?*" he said incredulously.

Fred gave Betty just the flicker of a grin, and then looked across the table at the banker. "I drive a bus in New York City," he said. "I'm a bus driver."

"Well, my goodness," said the banker, "that's marvelous! I've always envied the job you fellows do. Tell me, don't you ever lose your temper with all that traffic and all those people pushing and shoving?"

He wasn't being condescending or merely polite. His interest was completely genuine. And that was only the first question. Other guests joined in with real interest, real curiosity. And suddenly there was Fred the bus driver talking easily and naturally about his work with no hesitancy, no apology, no sense of inferiority. Norman looked at me and I looked at Norman and I think we both said a little prayer of thanksgiving. Because faith had worked a small miracle, as it so often does—and the faith that did it was Betty's.

She believed in her husband, until he believed in himself. It's the finest moment a woman can have in the adventure of being a wife. And Norman and I were never prouder of any friends we ever had.

The desire to protect a loved one from harm, to spare him pain or unhappiness, is an instinct almost as powerful as the instinct for self-preservation, I think, especially in women. In my own case, I have had the extra incentive of knowing that Norman's work has helped thousands—perhaps millions—of people to fight or grope their way to the religious faith that I consider the most important thing in life. So I have always done my very best to spare him needless worry, or any kind of upset that might interfere with his creativity or peace of mind.

Sometimes it's just a little thing. Not long ago, for example, the organ at the Marble Church broke down. (Incidentally, this was the first electrically operated pipe organ in the country and when it was first installed, people came for miles to hear an organ not pumped by hand.) The organist let me know the night before the Sunday services, adding that on a weekend nothing could be done about repairs. I could have told Norman right away; obviously he would have to know eventually. But I thought this minor problem might just be enough to take the edge off his final work in preparing his sermon.

So I said nothing until the very last minute before the service, when I knew the sermon was complete and fixed in his mind. He was a bit startled, but he didn't have time to worry about it. In fact, as I suspected, he turned it into a fun thing. "The faithful organ," he told the huge congregation, "after all these years has wheezed to a stop—at least temporarily. I'm told today we'll all have to sing *a cappella* —whatever that means!" Everyone laughed, and the *a cappella* singing was tremendous.

Sometimes, of course, a wife's best efforts to head off trouble fail. I remember vividly the time a national magazine decided to publish an article about religion in America in which certain churchmen said some very critical things about Norman's ministry. This included his books, with their common-sense approach to everyday problems. The editors sent a copy of the article to me for my reaction well in advance of publication. It seemed to me that the article was not only unfair, but it contained actual misstatements of fact. I told the editors this, but apparently they were less interested in a balanced and accurate presentation than in the extra circulation that might result from a controversial treatment. I was informed politely that, despite my objections, the article would appear in an early fall issue.

This was a time of real testing for me. I knew some of

these clergymen-critics personally, and served on various boards and committes with them. I knew that to carry out my responsibilities at these gatherings, I would have to continue to treat them as if nothing had happened. Believe me, this was hard to do. I spent days, literally days, praying to be free of bitterness. I think that finally, with God's help, I conquered it. At least, I was able to face them calmly and carry out unemotionally such business as we had to conduct.

I remember that in the case of one of these gentlemen, I felt his criticism contained errors of fact that amounted to untruths. So I wrote him a letter, pointing out these mistakes and asking him to retract them. He finally replied, saying that he was sorry if he was wrong, that he had heard these things at second- or third-hand. I think he would have made a retraction, but by that time it was too late. The article was already in production.

All this happened in the late spring. Norman and I were planning a trip to Europe where we hoped to work on a book. I knew that if he were aware of this Sword of Damocles hanging over his head, he would be so upset and distressed that any effective work would be impossible. In fact, the whole summer would be ruined.

Consequently I said nothing about the article, although I was deeply worried, not so much about its impact on the public (because I believed in their loyalty and fair-mindedness), as about its effect on Norman himself. It is a curious thing, but despite all the courage and strength he has given to thousands of unsure people, Norman himself remains at times a highly sensitive and vulnerable person. I knew that even though the criticisms leveled at him were unjust, he would be deeply distressed. I was afraid that he might even decide to resign from the church.

All that summer I lived with the burden of my unwelcome secret. I did my best to appear cheerful and unconcerned. This was difficult because Norman is highly intuitive and it is not easy to conceal any emotional crosscurrents from him. On top of all this, word reached us in Switzerland that Norman's father, whom we both loved dearly, was in poor health—that his condition might become serious at any time.

Right up to the end of the summer I said nothing about the article to Norman. But when we stepped off the ship that brought us home, the publication was on the newsstands. To make matters worse, there was a telegram from Norman's brother saying that his father was failing fast and could not live much longer. Norman immediately took a train to the town in upstate New York where his father was ill. On the train he read the article. It left him so upset and shaken that, as I feared, he wrote out his resignation from the church on the train that night.

Here, then, was a crisis that I had been able to postpone but not avoid. Now it was even worse than I had expected, because it was reinforced by the strain and worry of Father Peale's illness. Norman's two brothers were already at his father's bedside. When he told them of his decision to resign, and even showed them the letter he had written on the train, they tried to dissuade him, but he would not listen to them. All they could extract from him was a promise not to make a final decision until he had talked to me.

I knew without being told that everything depended on how I behaved. If I sympathized too much, Norman might find in such sympathy approval of what he intended to do. If I opposed his decision too strongly, he might brush aside my opposition as nothing but wifely loyalty. When I prayed for guidance—and I have never prayed harder in my life— the answer I seemed to get was, "Keep calm. Don't do anything extreme. Play for time."

So that is what I did. With as much calmness as I could muster, I accepted the fact that he had written out his resignation. I knew his own Marble Church people would be loyally supportive of him. It was the general church from which he wanted to separate himself. But I took the resignation and even made some editorial suggestions where the wording was concerned. I did not say that what he intended doing was foolish, or insist that he change his mind. I merely pointed out that a decision of such magnitude should not be made under stress. If he felt the same way in two weeks, I said, I would not oppose him. But I thought he owed it to his friends, his family, and himself—not to mention the millions who believed in him—to think about it and pray about it until he was sure that his mind was perfectly clear and his emotions under control. Finally, he agreed.

The whole thing was resolved in a strange and wonderful way. During this waiting period, Norman's father died. We went to the funeral. At the funeral, Norman's stepmother, Mary Peale, told him she had a message to give him, something his father had whispered to her before he died. She said that Norman's father had guessed that something was wrong, had sensed that the chorus of criticism was getting him down, had known that he was facing some sort of inner crisis. The message was: "The Peales never quit." His father said, "Let Norman know it would break my heart if he should ever quit. In fact," he added, "Norman is one hundred percent all right. Tell him for me to tell them to go to Hell."

When Norman heard that he wept, then laughed. "What a man our father is," he said. He took his resignation out of his pocket and handed it to me. "Tear it up," he said.

With thankfulness and relief, knowing that my prayers had been answered, I tore it up.

There are very few marriages, I'm sure, where this situation doesn't arise sooner or later, a situation in which one partner is threatened, upset, driven to extreme action that may or may not be wise. And this is precisely the time when the other partner can salvage or retrieve the situation by keeping calm, by praying for guidance, and above all by taking some of the shock, absorbing it, rolling with the punch until the worst of the crisis is over.

I remember very well the time in a midwestern city when we were staying in a very large hotel, one of the key properties in a very important hotel chain. We had stayed there before, and had become friendly with the assistant manager and his wife, both admirable people. On this occasion we got a telephone call from this man asking us to have lunch with him and his wife, saying they would like to talk to us. It was a personal matter, he said—and to them an important one.

I'll never forget how they looked when they came into the dining room. The man was pale, tense, obviously much upset. The woman was upset, too, but I could see that her whole concern was for her husband. She was not thinking about herself.

What had happened, it seemed, was that the manager of the hotel was retiring. This had been expected for some time, and the assistant manager had hoped that the job would be his. He had practically been told as much, he said, by a high official of the hotel chain. But that very morning word had come down that a manager was to be brought in from outside. Our friend was not to get the job after all. He was so disappointed, hurt, and angry, that he had decided to resign. He had been on the point of calling up his superiors and telling them just what he thought of them when his wife remembered that we were in the hotel. She had persuaded him to talk to us first.

Now, if anything, the wife was angrier than her husband. She loved him, believed in him, hated to see him hurt. Her first instinct, I'm sure, was to strike out at the thing that was hurting him—which in this case was the impersonal management of a great hotel chain.

But she also knew that at the moment her husband's judgment was impaired, that he was capable of doing something he might regret later. Also, the practical, sensible homemaker inside the angry wife knew that she and her husband were both middle-aged, that jobs as good as the one they had did not grow on trees, that they had two children to think about—one in college. She knew her man well enough to know that in his present state of mind nothing she could say would have much effect. But she also knew that he admired Norman and might listen to him. So here they were.

In a case like this, Norman never says much at first. He always encourages the person in trouble to pour it out, ventilate all the anger, the frustration, the bitterness, whatever (as he puts it) is "heating up the mind." So the assistant manager talked for some time, reviewing all his past contributions to the hotel, marshaling all the arguments why he was perfectly capable of taking over the top job, occasionally appealing to his wife for confirmation—which she always gave.

Finally, when he had talked himself out, Norman began to place "cool" ideas in the vacancies left by all the "hot" ones that had come sizzling out of the man. He started out by saying calmly that while this disappointment was hard to take, maybe God had some plan in mind for both of them and that this could be a part of that plan. He said he thought it would be very foolish, though understandable, for the man to quit his job in a fit of anger. "The work you do here is important," Norman said. "You make tired people comfortable. You make dispirited people cheerful. You're a warm, welcoming sort of person, and people sense that, and they like it. I think you're in the business God meant you to be in, even if the rung of the ladder you want is still out of reach."

The man stared at the tablecloth and said nothing, but I could see that he was listening.

"Now," said Norman, "you are an intelligent person and a big person, so I am going to make a suggestion that a small person or a stupid person could not follow. I suggest that you make yourself swallow your injured pride and your sense of injustice and treat the new manager with great courtesy and respect. As you know better than anyone, you can make his new assignment hard, or you can make it easy. I hope you will make it easy by cheerfully helping him in every way. After all, he hasn't done anything unfair. I don't think you should focus your resentment on him."

Then he turned to the wife. "And I have the same suggestion for you. Treat the new manager's wife as nicely as you possibly can. After all, she's in a difficult position too. Everyone will know that you hoped for the job, that you are deeply disappointed not to have it. Everyone will be watching for you to show resentment or hostility. Don't give them that satisfaction. Treat your new boss just the way you'd want him to treat you, if you were in his shoes."

I remember how the assistant made a wry face and gave a reluctant laugh. "I can see we made a mistake inviting you two to have lunch with us," he said. "You're telling us to act like Christians. And that's just the way we don't feel like acting."

Norman and I laughed, too, because we knew we had gotten through to him. Oh, he still took some convincing. But his wife swung around to our side (she had been there all along, really) and began to point out various ways in which he could be of enormous value to the new man. "You'll be a lot more important to him," she said, "than you were to our old boss, who knew all the ropes. I'll bet you'll have more responsibility, more authority than you've ever had before."

Which is exactly the way things worked out. The new manager was so grateful and so impressed that three years later, when he moved on to yet another job, he recommended our friend so highly that he moved into the top spot with no trouble at all.

There was a kind of postscript to the story, too. Norman happened to meet a man who was on the board of that hotel chain. The talk came around to our friend. "You know," the board member said, "the reason we didn't promote him the first time was that we weren't quite sure how he could handle himself under pressure. We were always afraid that in a tough situation he might let his emotions run away with him. But when he took that disappointment with so much grace and self-control, we decided we must be wrong about him." Then he gave Norman a suspicious look. "You didn't have anything to do with all that, did you?"

"His wife was the key," said Norman cheerfully. "She deserves the credit."

And of course, truly she did!

✣ 16 ✣

WHEN THE
SPARKS FLY

✣ Every minister's wife—and every minister too—knows that a lot of people tend to become solemn and pious when the preacher comes around. Everybody is suddenly on his best behavior. Everybody puts his best foot forward, with the result that at times nothing seems quite real!

Countless times, talking with a married couple I've just met, I've had them say to me, "Oh, yes, we've been married fifteen years (or twenty, or thirty) and we've never had a cross word between us." I always smile and nod happily, but what I'm really thinking is, "How dull! How boring! What a drag a marriage like that would be!"

I certainly don't want to imply that a bitter quarrel in marriage is a good thing. People say and do things in anger that can damage any relationship, sometimes permanently. But I do think that a disagreement between married partners can actually be constructive and useful if (and it's a big "if") it's handled in the right way.

Over the years, there have been plenty of areas where Norman and I were not in accord. There still are. I wouldn't think of agreeing with him on every subject! But we have learned certain dos and don'ts that tend to turn potential arguments into useful discussions.

One, for example, is the importance of easing up gradually on an area of disagreement, taking just a piece of it at first (the least explosive piece), discussing that aspect, then letting the matter rest for a while. We've found that if you nibble around the edges of an argument, instead of trying to bite off more than either of you can chew, you're likely to be able to digest the problem much better in the end. I heard a very successful business executive say once that when a touchy subject has to be dealt with in his board room, he tries to make sure that the discussion is conducted in slow motion. That's a pretty good rule for marital discussions, too.

Another technique that I have learned to value is simply the practice of silence at certain times. There are areas in arguments—and every married person recognizes them— where you suddenly realize that your partner is no longer talking about the issue at hand, but about something else that is highly charged with emotion. When this happens, the best thing to do is not to argue or counterpunch, but just let the other person talk himself out. As the old saying goes, silence is golden.

There are various other common-sense things that can take the sting out of marital disagreement if you can just keep them in mind: the importance of compromise (compromise doesn't mean giving in); the value of emphasizing the positive when making your case (negative arguments rarely influence anybody); the trick of trying—*really* trying —to put yourself in your adversary's shoes and seeing the issue from his point of view. All these guidelines are helpful, but it's surprising how many married people have never thought of them or tried to apply them. When disagreements arise, they just react with anger—and react again with more anger.

When young wives seek my advice in such matters, as they do quite frequently, I'm always amused at their as-

sumption that, being a minister's wife, I have never heard
an angry or unkind word from my husband and consequently don't know what a real husband-wife altercation is.
It's true that Norman and I almost never have any serious
differences nowadays, but this was not always the case.
When we were first married, Norman was a very young
man in a very demanding job. There were times when he
wondered if he was equal to the job (he was more than
equal to it, but he had a kind of basic insecurity that made
him worry anyway), and when the tension caused by this
reached a certain point, he could be very hard to live with.

All wives, to some extent, have to act as lightning rods,
but this is not the pleasantest role in the world, and in
those days I wasn't mature enough for it. So when Norman
was short-tempered or irritable, I had a tendency to flare
up in return, or else react with hurt feelings. When he was
sarcastic—and being a master of words he could put a real
sting into them—I would often try to strike back. But when
I did, he would remember what I had said in anger and
use my own words against me. Verbally, I was no match
for him.

The main lesson I learned from all this was that if I
wanted the battle or the black mood to end quickly, I had
to control myself. If I cut off the fuel by refusing to become
angry or fight back, the whole thing blew over much more
quickly.

Fortunately for me, there was a fundamental streak of
fairness in Norman that made him capable of admitting his
own failings now and then. I remember one time when he
was being his most objectionable self. I stood it as long as
I could. Then I took him into our bedroom and closed the
door so that the children couldn't hear me and really told
him off. "For once," I said furiously, "you are going to keep
still and listen to me. You're being mean and hateful, and

you know it. Those black moods of yours are your worst character defect, and yet you won't face up to this or try to change it!" I ranted and raved, but in the middle of my tirade I noticed that a strange expression had come over Norman's face. He didn't seem to be listening to me at all. In fact, as he told me later, he was having a very strange inner, or psychic, experience.

He said that as I talked, it suddenly seemed to him that he was very far away, standing on the bank of a stream. My voice seemed to come from a great distance; he could hear it only dimly. The vision, or whatever it was, was extraordinarily real. He could see the water swirling past, and suddenly, out in the middle of the stream, he became aware of a dark, formless, half-submerged object bobbing sullenly in the current. He knew, furthermore, that this object symbolized the element in his makeup that I was objecting to, that it was ugly and evil, and that somehow he had to break it up, get rid of it, deal with it so that it would be gone forever.

Usually in such a situation he would deny my accusations or defend his position, but now he simply said, "You're right. I'm a mean devil. I saw it, this thing—this meanness that you're talking about. I know I've got to get it out of my system."

From that moment on, he seemed to see himself in a different light. He didn't turn into a paragon overnight, but he was certainly easier to live with!

I think that in many marriages the first long step toward happiness comes with the realization that *everyone* has some unpleasant quirk or weakness, and that an important part of marriage consists in trying to balance or compensate for such eccentricities or failings in the person you're sharing your life with. It's a feeling of protectiveness, not just toward the other person but toward the marriage itself. It's a determination not to let the partnership be damaged, regardless of what the threat may be or where it comes from.

For example, I know one wife whose husband is a compulsive spender. He throws money around, partly because he's a generous person, partly because, being somewhat insecure, he wants people to like him and thinks that they will if he always picks up the check. He can't afford this kind of extravagance, but he can't seem to help it.

The wife knows that she can't oppose this tendency in her husband directly; she has tried and failed. And so she opposes it indirectly. She avoids restaurant gatherings, saying she prefers to eat at home. If she and her husband go to a baseball game or to the movies with another couple, she will often give the other wife the money for her own and her husband's ticket in advance, thus heading off any grand gesture on her husband's part. He teases her good-naturedly about being a tightwad, but everyone who knows them is aware that she is simply protecting their marriage and their life together—and in so doing is performing the basic function of a loving wife.

Most young wives will find, as they grow older and wiser, that they can almost never change objectionable or undesirable characteristics in their husbands by frontal assault. Angry recriminations just make matters worse. The only approach that works is rational discussions in moments of calmness, appeals to fair-mindedness, or quiet demonstrations of how hurtful or unwise the negative or objectionable quality really is.

I knew one young wife—I'll call her Mrs. Harrison—who married into a very close-knit family. They were not only very fond of one another, they were all great talkers. Whenever there was a family gathering, this combination of affection and fluency became overwhelming. Nobody else could get a word in edgewise. Guests just had to sit there, mute and helpless. The members of the family were so interested in one another, and in family activities, anecdotes, jokes, and reminiscences, that the rest of the world and the people in it didn't exist for them.

Some new wives might have accepted this situation with resignation. Some might have smouldered in silence. But this was a forthright girl, so she decided to take it up with her husband. "Darling," she said (always a good word to begin a discussion with!), "I don't think any of you realize it, but when you Harrisons get together you're really quite rude. You don't show even polite interest in what anyone outside the family might have to say. You just turn them off."

"Oh, come now," the husband said, "you're being hypersensitive, aren't you? You know perfectly well we're always delighted to hear anything you have to say. All you have to do is speak up!"

"I do try to speak up," she told him. "And I've heard other people try. But it's hopeless. If we attempt to tell a story, one of you always tops it with one of your own. Or else it reminds you of some family episode that you just have to tell about. And the worst of it is that you're not even aware that you're doing it!"

"I still think you're exaggerating," her husband said cheerfully. "We can't be as bad as all that."

The young wife said no more, but she went out and rented a battery-powered tape recorder. At the next family gathering she hid the machine in one of the compartments of the sideboard and recorded the whole dinner-table conversation. That night, when she and her husband were alone, she played the tape, stopping it occasionally to insert her own comments ("Now here's Jim's wife trying feebly to talk about her own college days; notice how your mother cuts her off." Or, "This is me, trying to speak up the way you told me I should. See how far I get!")

The husband, utterly amazed, called a family conference

of his parents and brothers and sisters and played the tape
for them, adding some of the comments his wife had made.
Everyone was astounded. Fortunately, being a warmhearted
as well as a conversation-monopolizing group, they took no
offense but honestly tried to mend their ways and succeeded,
as my friend said dryly, "part of the time, anyway."

Sometimes a sharp quarrel that clears the air is better
than a sullen deadlock that drags on and on. And I have
known of cases where a married pair quarreled so violently
and hit bottom so hard that they were shaken into a new
and better relationship.

There was a couple in Florida, typical young-marrieds,
who had this experience. Their troubles began when the
husband received a promotion and they moved into a suburb where the residents considered themselves the local
jet set. The young pair stopped going to church, because
none of their new friends went to church. They started to
drink more than was good for them. They began to quarrel
and bicker about trifles. Their marriage was drifting toward
the rocks.

One night at a country-club dance where everyone had
been drinking heavily, a man who had recently been divorced began to make obvious advances to the young wife.
It seemed to the husband that, far from discouraging these
advances, his wife actually welcomed them and led the man
on. He dragged her from the party, and flung her into their
car and drove home, berating her bitterly. She replied in
kind. By the time they reached their house, they were both
wild with anger. As they got out of the car in their garage,
the wife said something so infuriating that her husband lost
all self-control and struck her, knocking her to the concrete
floor.

She lay there, crumpled like a broken flower, a trickle of
blood running down her chin. The man stared down at her,
horrified, all the anger draining out of him. He fell on his

knees and gathered her in his arms. "Oh, God," he cried. "God help us!"

"Yes," the wife said brokenly, "we need Him to help us. We need to get back to Him before it's too late." Clinging together they sobbed and prayed. And because in this extremity they had Someone to turn to, Someone all-powerful and all-compassionate, they were able to climb out of the pit they had dug for themselves and become friends and lovers once more.

Friends and lovers—when that balance is achieved in marriage, and survives all the storms and stresses, nothing in the world brings so much happiness and so much joy.

❦ 17 ❦

LIVING OUT
OF A
SUITCASE

❦ I spend at least one-fourth of my time away
from home. Norman's work takes him into all parts of
the country and the world on speaking engagements and
other duties. At first glance this may sound exciting and
adventurous, but it means living out of a suitcase, and believe me, this requires adjustment.

Norman says that I am the world's best packer, and
that I can get more in a suitcase than anybody he ever heard
of and all without a wrinkle. Many a time we have gone
to Europe with two suitcases and not overly large ones at
that. And we have gone around the world with three bags
containing enough clothes to be ready for all kinds of occasions: dinners, receptions, sporting events, other functions.

I recall vividly the departure scene for a family trip with
our three children many years ago. We were going to visit
all of the National Parks and see as much of the United
States as possible. We wanted our children to know and
love the United States before they started wandering over
any other part of the world.

It had been agreed that each person could have one
suitcase. For the children this meant clothes for hiking,
horseback riding, tennis, as well as dress clothes for evening
dinner in the hotels and on the train. (Those were the days

when practically all travel was by sleeper train. I have always been thankful for this experience because really it is the only way to see the vastness and variety and beauty of our great land.)

The evening of departure arrived and all five bags were neatly placed at the door. Norman rushed in from the office, having worked until the last moment, which is always his habit. "You're not going to take all those bags, are you?" he exclaimed. And we were going to be gone a month!

My husband comments that after I have been in a hotel room for thirty minutes it has been converted into a home. I completely unpack and put everything neatly into drawers even if it is only a one-night stand. I stow the suitcases out of sight just as if we were going to stay a month. With pictures of the family around, familiar articles on the dresser, the alarm clock available, and books and magazines on an end table, the room is soon a home.

As I just mentioned, our whole family has traveled together throughout the United States, in Europe, the Middle East, the Far East, and South America. These experiences have done much toward establishing a deep feeling of rapport in our family. And of course, Norman and I have traveled together, just the two of us, to many fabulous and exciting places, the South Seas, Australia, Indonesia, Arabian Gulf from Calcutta to Baghdad, to the fabled coasts of Spain and elsewhere along the highways to romance.

We have been through the stage of our teen-agers wanting to travel by themselves. Although we weren't overly enthusiastic about this we felt it was part of their developing experience and always encouraged them. John hitchhiked through Europe one summer and lost at least twenty pounds. Other summers he worked in a fishing village in

Scotland, a work camp in France, and a farm in Switzerland.

Margaret traveled through Europe with her college roommate by car, train, and plane. She also spent a summer in a work camp in France. Our youngest daughter, Elizabeth, spent two summers in a French school in Villar, Switzerland called LaHarpe. Only French was spoken here. When we questioned her about the advantages of such restrictions she said, "Well, I found out that my French teacher in New York speaks French with a Brooklyn accent!"

Perhaps the most difficult experience for Norman and me was the day when we saw our three children take off from Frankfurt to Moscow, alone. They were going behind the Iron Curtain. We knew we could not communicate with them and probably they would get nothing out to us. There was a long silence between us as we watched the plane disappear like a speck in the sky. What a happy reunion some three weeks later at the Zurich airport when they piled off the plane loaded with caviar and fur hats.

One of the things I regret most in my far-from-blameless life is my failure to keep a diary. Norman and I have been to so many wonderful places, seen so many wonderful sights, met so many fascinating people that not keeping some kind of daily record seems almost like criminal negligence. I have no alibi to offer—except that when your days are as full as ours tend to be, it requires almost superhuman self-discipline to make yourself sit down at the typewriter and record impressions while they're still vivid. And I'm very human.

One thing I have done, though, is try to keep in touch with family and business associates by writing fairly detailed letters when we're away from home. This also preserves a sense of unity with our children. Twice in recent years our travels have taken us right around the globe. I've already described our last visit to Taiwan, so I needn't repeat any of that. But some of the letters I wrote from other places may be of interest. At least our children were kind enough to say they were, and to keep them.

In re-reading these letters I find an astonishing amount of detail. But this, I think, is because in our travels I have tried to make myself as receptive as possible, to focus on small things, to absorb sights and sounds and smells so that the memories will be as vivid as possible and last for years. I think this is a matter of self-training. Any wife, whether she's a world traveler or a stay-at-home can learn to sharpen her powers of observation and in the process heighten her enjoyment of the adventure of being a wife.

Some people, I know, are less interested in travel and foreign lands than others. These readers may not wish to follow me as I re-live some of our recent journeys in the Far East and India. To them I say cheerfully, you have my blessing if you wish to skip to page 185 where the letters end and my narrative begins again.

So here are a few selected letters just as I wrote them from far-away places in this fascinating world of ours.

Enroute Bullet train from Tokyo to Kyoto

Dear Family,

We are aboard the famous fast train of Japan that is supposed to go up to 160 miles an hour. It hasn't done so yet, and Norman hopes it won't! It makes only one stop in our journey of approximately 300 miles. The cars are extra wide, with picture windows on each side. There is practically no vibration and no swing. It is really fantastic.

Seven hours and seventeen minutes after takeoff from Honolulu we touched the runway in Tokyo. This is now the largest city in the world—over

11,000,000 people. It has always been busy, noisy, and confusing, but is more so these days. New buildings are everywhere and more are under construction. The old restriction about height is no more, so skyscrapers are springing up all over downtown Tokyo. Traffic is perhaps even worse than New York, even though many superhighways have been built.

Japan is now second to the United States in gross national product, having passed West Germany. And I predict that unless we in the United States learn again the art of working, Japan will pass us. Excellence seems to be the key word. Service is a privilege. There is no tipping.

Now for some of our experiences. Armin H. Meyer, the American Ambassador to Japan, invited us to the Embassy for tea. This official residence is known as Hoover's Folly, for it was built in 1932 at the height of the Depression when almost no public buildings were being authorized. But it is a beautiful place.

He invited us to go with him to a baseball game the next evening to see the Tokyo Giants play the Osaka Tigers. We sat in the President's box and it reminded us of the many times we sat with Branch Rickey in the Executive box in the old Dodger stadium in Brooklyn. The Giants lost, but it was a superb game and made us wonder why we think we Americans should have a monopoly on the "World Series"! The Tigers have two Americans on their team, and one of them hit a home run. The stands went wild. Just under the scoreboard, fountains began to play and bells started to ring. The Japanese seem to have a lot more imagination than we have.

Student unrest is everywhere. We seem to think it is only in the United States, but Tokyo University with sixteen thousand students has been closed for one year. The student demands sound just like those in America.

The snow is gone from Mt. Fuji. This is our fourth trip to Japan, but the mountain has always been in clouds before. What a thrill to see it this time.
Our love to everyone.

Ruth

Manila, Philippines

Dear Family,

We learned that the airport in Manila was to be closed at the time of our scheduled arrival because President Nixon was arriving and security had closed airport to all commercial planes for four hours.
We quickly changed our flight plans to early morning and arrived at about 9:30 A.M. along with typhoon "Viola." The wind was blowing a gale and continued for all our time in Manila. Sunshine was interspersed with the most torrential rains I have ever seen. It was like waving sheets or curtains. One good feature was that it did not rain continually and you could wait it out.

The city was gaily decorated. Already people were gathering at the airport to welcome President and Mrs. Nixon. All along the route into the city flags were flying, adults and school children lined the sidewalks, big white arches built over the highway proclaimed welcome, and large pictures of Richard Nixon with the sign MABUHAY at the tops were everywhere. This means the same thing as "Aloha" in Honolulu or "Welcome" in America.

Our friends Fely and Jimmie Go (Mr. Go is publisher of the *Fookien Times*) called soon after our arrival at the hotel, and Fely said she would come right over. We had been invited to the State Dinner for the Nixons that night, and needed to have formal evening dress. My first thought was that I had brought along Norman's barong tagalog, an elaborately embroidered, long-sleeved organdy shirt that is worn outside the trousers for evening wear with no jacket. But what would I do for a long dress?

Fely arrived, looked at Norman's shirt, and said it was not elaborate enough and was too old-fashioned! I had bought it in the Philippines twelve years ago. Well, we went to her favorite shop, found a Filipino banana fibre dress with big butterfly sleeves and all-over embroidery that I stepped right into. It needed only slight alterations. Then she went to the men's department, picked out a shirt length that was already embroidered for front, back, collar, cuffs, and sleeves, and ordered it made—both garments to be delivered to our room at the hotel not later than four P.M. that day! And they were there. Luckily, I had evening shoes, bag, kid gloves, and jewelry, so all was well.

The State Dinner was at the famous Malacanan Palace. We entered the Palace grounds, beautifully festooned with lights—along the driveway, all over the trees and shrubs, and outlining the roofs and windows of the Palace. It was a fairyland of lights.

Finally, we were ushered into the State dining room, brilliantly lighted by crystal chandeliers, with a very long head table and eight-person round tables for all other guests. We were seated near the front center. Each table was decorated with five-branched candelabra set amid flowers and the flags of the two countries. Each guest received a memento in the form

of a heavy medallion with the profiles of Presidents
Marcos and Nixon on one side and their official seals
on the other.

One society matron was heard to say, "I've been to
five State Dinners. This one tops them all." Mrs.
Marcos supervised the menu herself. It was: Goose
Liver Pâté, Palawan Turtle Soup, Coquille of King
Lapu-lapu (fish), Mindanao Pigeon Tropicale, Delice
Patricia (a dessert of mango scooped from its shell
and replaced after being mixed with mango ice cream
and nuts, capped with a wafer topped with a sugar
rose and surrounded with whipped cream). Was it
good! And so beautiful to look at! Petit Fours and
coffee finished the repast.

Martial music indicated that President and Mrs.
Marcos and President and Mrs. Nixon were arriving.
Everyone stood until they were seated. Then we
started on the dinner I have just described. Looking
across the room Mrs. Nixon recognized me, and a look
of unbelief crossed her face. Then she smiled and
threw me a kiss. Later during the dinner, Secretary of
Foreign Affairs Carlos P. Romulo came to our table
and said that Mrs. Marcos wanted to meet Dr. Peale,
as she reads all his books. So he was escorted to the
head table, met them all and had a nice visit with
President and Mrs. Nixon. The President complimented Norman on his beautiful barong, suggesting
it might hang better if he were more slender.

After dinner everyone went through the Palace
garden, past exhibits of native arts and crafts, and
into a large hall set up for an entertainment. It was
very crowded because twice as many had been invited to this part of the evening as to the State
Dinner. The two Presidents and their wives were on
a slightly raised platform at one end of the room, and

the entertainment went on opposite this raised area. All the seats were occupied when we got to this hall, and we were standing at the side. Presently the American Ambassador came up to where we were standing and said that Mrs. Marcos would like us to come up on the platform and sit with them. So, believe it or not, we sat in the seats of honor along with the two Presidents and their wives.

The program consisted of music and group singers and a wonderful exhibit of native dancing by the Bayanihan dance troupe.

The end of the program was clearly intended to be a surprise. It was a tableau staged by the famous Filipino producer, Bert Aveliana. Philippine troops and U.S. Marines marched in with the national colors of both countries, and the panels in the backdrop for the program slid open to reveal two live scenes: A Filipino soldier supporting a wounded American and another Filipino trooper being treated by an American medic.

In the background the Madrigal singers hummed "Philippines, My Philippines" and "Battle Hymn of the Republic," then led the entire crowd in singing the two national anthems. It was one of the most moving experiences of my life.

The rest of our stay in Manila was governed largely by "Viola." The storm canceled our trip into the mountains, and we left Manila for Hong Kong a day early.

But before leaving, Norman preached at the Central United Methodist Church, the same one where his mother preached nearly forty-five years ago. For him this was a moving experience and there was a huge audience. One of his college classmates, Leonardo Padilla, introduced him. Many people spoke of reading his books and sermons and also *Guideposts*. It is really fascinating so far from home to find so many friends.

Our love to everyone.

Ruth

Hong Kong

Dear Family and Everyone:

In my last letter I indicated that we left Manila one day early because typhoon "Viola" prevented us from going to the Country Club up in the mountains at Baguio. We were sorry to miss this because we understand it is very beautiful. However, we were not loath to have an extra day in Hong Kong, the shopping mecca of the world!

Typhoon "Winnie" met us there, but it was not nearly as bad as "Viola." We were astounded at the new buildings in Hong Kong. Much public housing has been built, many apartments have gone up, and in one area Mobil Oil is building cooperative apartments to house seventy thousand people. Stage one in this development is finished and fully occupied and stage two is in construction.

Our room in the Mandarin Hotel overlooked Hong Kong harbor, and it was a constantly changing scene. Some naval vessels, both American and British, were always in sight. Luxury passenger ships came into the docks for two or three days and then left. Ships from Communist China came loaded with produce. These anchored in the harbor, and junks came alongside to unload the cargo and take it to the vegetable and fish markets on shore.

A junk is a Chinese boat on which a whole family lives and works. Sometimes a family will own a junk and a sampan. This latter is a smaller boat used mainly for fishing. Sometimes one would see as many as six or eight junks around a big freighter, taking off cargo and loading other cargo. Hong Kong is flooded with goods from Communist China, and some of it is excellent workmanship. The U.S. restrictions have been eased and each tourist can bring $100 worth of goods made in Communist China into the United States. I bought some beautiful embroidered Swatow linen from Kwong Tung Province and two figures from the Ming Dynasty that are over 200 years old. And I was tempted by a lot more, but had reached my limit.

We had dinner in two private homes in Hong Kong. Mr. and Mrs. Paul Braga, who have worshipped in Marble Collegiate Church many times, are wonderful friends. He is an Englishman who has been in the automobile business in Hong Kong for many years. They have a beautiful home with a breathtaking view of the city. Our other hostess was Mrs. Pola Lee, who has two children studying in the United States and plans to come to New York herself this winter. This home is exquisite beyond description. It is perfectly air-conditioned. From an entrance hall you go down two steps into a large living room where one wall is entirely glass and looks into a lovely garden.

This living room is beautifully furnished with the same kind of furniture we all have at home: davenport, occasional chairs, coffee table, end tables, piano, lamps, etc. The thing that really made it different was this: As you looked around your eye was caught over and over again by a piece of beautiful porcelain, an intricately carved ivory base for a lamp, a silver box set with semi-precious stones, an ancient scroll, a painting that surely came out of old China. There was not too much, and everything was just right for its place.

Fourteen sat down for luncheon at a big round table with the usual chopsticks and lazy Susan. After the soup course all the serving dishes were placed on the lazy Susan and everyone served himself: frogs' legs, whitefish, beef, sweet and sour pork, mushrooms, string beans, etc., etc. Besides all this, each person was served a bowl of rice. We ate and ate and everything was delicious. When all of the serving dishes are put on the table at once instead of each course being served separately it means family-style, and the guests have been accepted into the family circle which in China is a great compliment to the guests.

Then came dessert, a huge bowl or basket of fresh fruit. Most of it was whole fruit like peaches, plums, bananas, etc. But a new kind of fruit had been peeled and prepared in quarters like sections of orange or grapefruit. It is called pamelo and we enjoyed it with such enthusiasm that our hostess asked the maid to bring a whole fruit so we could see it. It is about the size and color of grapefruit but slightly larger and the meat is coarser. Isn't this just as we would do at home? It was an unforgettable luncheon.

Hong Kong days were a series of luncheons, dinners, shopping, conferences, sight-seeing, and more shopping. Norman preached at the China Congregational Church on Sunday. His talk was, of course, interpreted. The church was packed and the officers, including some additional invited guests, gave a luncheon for us following the church service. Except for the food, it was just like any church family dinner and made us feel that Christian fellowship is the same the world over.

One of the highlights of our stay was a visit with Gladis and Gordon DePree who are Reformed Church missionaries in Hong Kong. This young couple with their three children have moved into a small fishing village and have identified completely with the simple village people. We walked through the market, stopped to speak with the shopkeepers, asked about the children, passed the time of day, etc. The DePrees have learned the language, and you can see that the people love them. He is teaching in one of the English schools and will become Headmaster within a year. More in next letter.

Love,

Ruth

Enroute to India

Dear Family,

The American Consul General in Hong Kong lives in a beautiful house high on a hill that commands a magnificent view of the entire harbor. It is on the Hong Kong side. We were invited to an afternoon reception where we met officials from England, New Zealand, and Finland, and during the afternoon I got some great shopping tips. Also, they were getting ready to receive Secretary of State Rogers and Mrs. Rogers the next day.

Hong Kong is an exciting city and one never wants to leave. Our visit of almost a week went very fast and we were sorry when it was over. But there was much ahead, especially Norman's trip to Viet Nam.

When our plane set down in Bangkok, a military car was waiting at the foot of the steps and as soon as the passport formalities were taken care of, we were driven out on the apron to an Air Force jet which was ready for takeoff. Colonel Hans E. Sandrock was there, having come all the way from Washington. Brigadier General Gerhardt W. Hyatt had come from Viet Nam to meet Norman. He is head of all the chaplains in Viet Nam. The three got aboard and left me alone! Of course the military took me to the hotel and were very kind and thoughtful all the time Norman was away.

Now I want to tell you about Bangkok. It is a city of contrasts: dazzling wealth and great poverty. The story, *The King and I*, took place here. The palace grounds and the temple areas really defy description because we have nothing with which to compare them. Gold is very plentiful and the temple buildings are covered with gold, so much so that you think it surely must be brass. But it isn't; it is gold. And colorful mosaics provide a vivid contrast to the gold. The Emerald Buddha is the focal point in one temple, the Reclining Buddha in another, and The Golden Buddha in a third. This latter is several tons of pure gold!

One day I took a trip on the Chao Phraya River and up the Klongs. These are canals or smaller rivers that wind for miles and on which one whole part of Bangkok life takes place. The Klongs are beehives of activity. Over one hundred thousand residents of Bangkok live on these waterways, and boats ply the Klongs to service these residents: vegetable boats, merchandise boats like floating department stores, restaurant boats, meat-market boats, etc.

Most of the houses along the water are shacks built on stilts driven right into the river bank. Sometimes a Buddhist temple appears on the bank between the

houses. Once in a while a beautiful home is seen
among the shacks. Living is right out in the open, for
one can look right into each house. We saw dishes
being washed at the river's edge, babies and children
being bathed, washing being done, even adults taking
a bath. The Klong water is indescribably dirty and
filled with refuse. We all had bananas as we rode
along in our boat, and our guide told us to throw the
peel overboard for the fish!

We saw many TV sets and one very elaborate
portable radio. Two homes had beautiful embroidered
pillowcases hanging on the drying rack and one had
embroidered curtains. I saw one pair of baby rubber
pants on a line. Some children were nude, some wore
shorts, some were very well-dressed in shirts and
pants. All were clean.

Huge earthen jars stood at each front door to catch
rainwater, an absolute necessity for each family. We
saw one man bathing out of one (with the aid of a
small vessel for dipping water out of the jar and
splashing it over himself). But most washing and
bathing is done right in the Klong.

Every shack and house had flowers. Orchids were
everywhere. House after house had a row of orchid
plants on the railing of what we would call the front
porch. Palm trees, banana trees, breadfruit trees,
oleanders, hibiscuses, and many other varieties of trees
and bushes lined the Klong. We passed many ship-
building and lumber yards where much activity was
going on. Children waved. A woman in a vegetable-
and-fruit boat came alongside and sold us the
bananas I mentioned. These boats are small and most
of them are manned by women. They are propelled
by a single oar manipulated from the rear end of the
boat. Sometimes a second woman sits in the front of

the boat and arranges and sells the vegetables while the other woman sculls. Both restaurant boats we saw were manned by women. A friend told me that a meal would cost about five cents and would consist of rice or noodles, a vegetable, and a little meat with gravy or sauce.

There is no winter in Bangkok and people do not feel poverty-stricken. Fruits and vegetables are abundant and very cheap. A native could buy a dress for $1.00. One American woman who has lived in Bangkok for many years told me that many women she knows live in very humble houses, but have the most elaborate and gorgeous wardrobes you could imagine. They don't put money in a place to live, but they all have servants and plenty of clothes.

I had lunch with Mrs. Robert Lewis in the Su Co Tai restaurant and we were the only Americans there. It is run by a woman who started in a very small way with a favorite recipe which so many people enjoyed that her friends urged her to make it available. The place has been enlarged many times and was packed the day we were there. Success is no different in Bangkok than in New York! Another guest at lunch that day was Mrs. Sirat Tantrakun (Golden), a famous singer who entertained when the King gave his State Dinner for the Nixons on their recent visit.

Now I don't know whether to share the next with you or not. I went to a boxing match! It was "Suek Payak Chaiyo" boxing at the Lumpinee Stadium in Bangkok. I will try to describe it as seen from our ringside seats. As each contestant enters he goes to his corner and strikes a pose as in meditation. One would think he is offering a prayer, but it is part of a ceremony that is a tribute to his teacher. Then each man comes near the center of the ring, kneels down, and with hands on the floor in front of him, bows his head on his hands and stays quiet for a full minute. Then, still staying on his knees, he raises up and very slowly bows several times.

Next, each man gets to his feet and prances around, making movements with his arms and hands that look as if they had some religious significance. Finally, the contest starts and the surprise begins. Nothing is barred. They box with their hands; they kick with their feet; they punch with their knees; they jab with their elbows to the side, the stomach, the legs, the face, the head. And they are always trying to throw each other to the floor.

The crowd goes wild. A drum and cymbal keep beating all the time. The constant noise is almost deafening. But it stops between rounds. The referee gets a terrible workout. Only a few women are in the crowd. The men are tense and excited—they bet, yell, jump up and down, clap each other on the back. It's amazing.

I visited a grocery store and saw all kinds of familiar items: Campbell soups, Del Monte fruits, Kraft mayonnaise, Wish-Bone French dressing (which I like and cannot buy in Pawling!), Hunt's tomato sauce, meat tenderizers, etc.

Last, but not least, we had a meeting with the entire business and editorial staff for the Thai edition of *Guideposts*. They are publishing just four issues a year, but are very encouraged with the reception and are gaining subscriptions slowly. They lack staff for a good promotion job, and I have some suggestions to make.

You can be sure that I was at the airport when Norman's Air Force jet touched down from Viet Nam.

It was a great reunion. But there was no time for him to rest. We had lunch with various military people and then went to call on the two generals in Bangkok. Later that day we had dinner at the home of General and Mrs. Wagstaff.

The Army never lets you rest. They planned a seven A.M. breakfast for all officers on the Bangkok base and then rushed us to a nine A.M. departure flight for India. And the Army never lets you do such mundane things as handle your own passports or boarding passes. They took care of it all, and we *drove* to the steps of the plane where all our credentials were returned to us and we waved goodbye.

Love,

Ruth

India

Dear Family,

India! I hardly know where to begin and frankly, I cannot write a happy story.

Coming into Calcutta we were told that 30,000 people sleep on the streets every night. This seemed such an overwhelming statement that I put it down as an exaggeration and waited to see for myself. After arrival in the city I asked an Indian and was told that this was an understatement—that perhaps the figure was nearer 50,000, and it ended up being 100,000! The dirt, the filth, the poverty, the human misery, the unsanitary conditions, the crowding, the children *everywhere*, defy description.

In Calcutta thousands of refugees have come from Pakistan trying to find work. Also, thousands of men come into the city from the rural areas because the land will not support the large families that are to be found everywhere in India. Much industry has developed in the cities, but it is not enough and unemployment is evident on every hand. We were told that the average wage of a worker in Calcutta was about $30 a month.

Our guide in Calcutta told us that the overwhelming problem of India is birth control. The first five-year plan of the government since independence was almost canceled out because the birthrate increased 2½ percent to 3 percent and thus the gains in employment, industrial development, etc., were to no avail.

India is a nation of villages; 87 percent of the people live in villages. Here houses are built of mud with no windows and one door. Most of them look as though they have one room. The streets are mud. There are no sanitary facilities and usually only one village well where all come to draw water. This must serve for all purposes, unless the family wash is done in the few ponds one sees occasionally. Almost everyone—men, women, and children—goes barefoot and lots of children are completely naked. The children and the men go to the bathroom along the roadways, or in the streets, or in the fields. They assume a squatting position and are perfectly oblivious of their surroundings or the people who pass by. Don't ask me about the women! At least they are not seen in public. But the idea of an outhouse has not penetrated this civilization.

You can imagine the smells, the unwashed bodies, the caked feet, the uncombed-unwashed heads, the dirty children, the clothes which may get infrequent washings, but in such dirty water that the cloth looks grimy.

It takes a great deal to throw me, but I feel discouraged about India. And yet, we have a powerful
lot of filth and dirt right in New York in streets that
are never cleaned.

Added to all this is the superstition that accom-
panies the Hindu religion. The cow is sacred and is
never to be harmed in any way. Cows roam the
streets at will and add to the traffic hazard along
with bicycles, cycle-cabs, oxen-drawn carts, people
walking, people carrying heavy burdens on their
heads, shoulders, and backs and trucks, buses, and a
few private cars. I have seen cows wandering in the
midst of the heaviest traffic in the very center of
Calcutta. A U.S. Government man was in jail four days
because his jeep grazed the side of a young calf in
traffic. We asked an Indian friend what would happen
to him if he killed a cow on the highway. He said he
probably would be mobbed and how badly he was
treated might depend upon his own attitude toward
the cow.

Farmers keep cows giving milk pretty well con-
fined and feed them pretty well. But the cows that
are not fresh are allowed to roam, and everyone is
supposed to feed them. You will see them going
from shop to shop. Of course the cow dung adds to
all the rest of the filth.

At Benares we visited the sacred Ganges River.
The great yearning of every Hindu is to visit the
Ganges once in his lifetime, to bathe in the sacred
river. We left our hotel at six one morning and proceeded directly to the edge of the water, descending
the famous steps leading down to the river and
entering into small boats—seven to a boat with a
guide and a rower. These boats proceeded slowly
along the water's edge and we watched the bathers.

Pilgrims must come early in the morning without partaking of any food. They step into the water—some fully dressed, some men with only loincloths, small children with no clothes at all. Some were very reverent and could be seen saying prayers, going through certain rituals, sipping water from the cupped hand or placing it on certain parts of the body as one would holy water. Others seemed to be just bathing, while some were actually washing clothes.

Some were in deep meditation and we saw several "Holy Men" who were sitting motionless, cross-legged, hands at ease in the lap, and eyes staring straight ahead. We got some good pictures, I believe. We saw one "Holy Man" who had covered himself from head to foot, including his face, with ashes and he looked like death itself. He had nothing on but a small loincloth and his long hair was wound on top of his head like a woman's.

After rowing up the river for about an hour we turned around and went in the other direction and finally came to the Burning Ghats. Here is another sacred place. All Hindus hope to bring their dead to the Ganges River where the bodies are burned and the ashes thrown in the sacred river.

I will try to explain the process. Hindus do not believe in embalming dead bodies. Within one or two hours of the person's being declared dead by the physician, relatives and friends start the long journey to the Ganges. Some come walking as far as one hundred miles. Only the male members of the family accompany the body, but other relatives and neighbors may go. We saw several such bands of people on the highways in and around Benares.

After reaching the Ganges, the dead body is dipped into the water of the holy river with the idea of purifying it. Then it is placed for some time on the steps of the Burning Ghat so that all the water may drain away from the body. Then it is wrapped in the same clothes which covered it for the journey. We saw one corpse wrapped in bright red cloth and were told it was a wife.

The next step is to build the pyre with wood logs. Then the chief mourner shaves his head clean and changes his old, used clothing to a new, white cloth. The body is placed on top of the pyre and the chief mourner goes to a higher level and gets a torch from the eternal fire and lights the pyre.

To kill bad odor and to facilitate burning, incense powder and sterilized butter are spread on the pyre. Generally it takes three to four hours for a body to be burned to ashes. The chief mourner is the next of kin—or the eldest son—or the one to inherit the estate. Many times disputes arise right at the Burning Ghat as to who is to start the pyre. When all is consumed the ashes are thrown by the relatives into the Ganges River. When we passed by the Burning Ghats two bodies were burning and one was being started. They say an average of fifty bodies are burned each day.

Death is never taken by the average Hindu as a terror. According to Hindu belief, the real man is not his physical body but his soul. And there being no death of the soul, no man actually dies. The dignified silence and peaceful appearance of the attendants reflect that feeling most vividly. Also, the Hindus believe in reincarnation—many, many times. So a loved one lives on, reincarnated.

At Benares we spent one day driving to Allahabad to see the Agricultural Institute which is run interdenominationally as a Christian institution. The president is our friend Dr. Ben Chitambar. We had a delightful luncheon in the home of the Chitambars. At the institute over 500 students, about one fourth women, are studying crops, soil, cattle, farm implements, domestic science, etc. In their research department they have developed a new plow which may eventually revolutionize the work of the farmer. Today, all over India, the land is plowed with a wooden plow drawn by a team of oxen, just as has been done since the beginning of time. This plow makes a 4-inch furrow and just that—does not turn over the soil or anything. There has been no change in this in centuries.

The Institute's research department made a steel plow that cuts a 12-inch furrow and turns the soil over at the same time. It is small and can be pulled by a team of oxen with the farmer following behind. These plows can be made for $3.50 so every farmer could eventually afford one. They hope to go into mass production. The plant manager told us he could sell 250,000 plows at once if they could be produced.

This letter has been written under duress and in many different sittings. The pace of travel has been accelerated and I have tried to write on planes and at odd moments, but it has not been easy. I will close now so there will be no further delay in getting some word to all the family.

Love,

Ruth

Much as we have traveled abroad, we travel even more at home. This may not be as exciting as travel abroad, but it lends variety and flavor and generates an ever-increasing pride in the sweep and grandeur of America. Norman has spoken repeatedly in forty-nine states, every state in the

United States except Alaska. He and I together crisscross the nation constantly, from one speaking engagement to another. But like a kind of spiritual homing pigeon, Norman is always back in the pulpit of the Marble Collegiate Church each Sunday morning.

One Monday, for example, we were in Louisville, where Norman addressed a big dinner, two thousand members of the Kentucky Bankers Association. Among other engagements, we went to a luncheon in honor of the eightieth birthday of our friend Colonel Harlan Sanders, of Kentucky Fried Chicken fame. Norman sat between the white-goateed Colonel and Governor Nunn of Kentucky. The main course, naturally, was Kentucky Fried Chicken. When Norman and the Governor started eating with knife and fork, the Colonel set them right. The way to eat his chicken, he said, was by hand—because it was "finger-lickin' good." So we all did—and it seemed to taste better!

On Tuesday we were in Dallas, where Norman spoke before a convention of cosmetic sales managers. There were about three thousand women in the audience, and perhaps twenty-five men. Norman always says he'd rather speak to men, or to a mixed audience, than to a lot of women. When you try to pin him down as to why, he becomes a little vague and mumbles that he never knows what feminine reactions to his humor are going to be. But in Dallas the ladies seemed to like him fine . . . especially the story about the reluctant schoolboy who was called upon to write a thumbnail biography of Benjamin Franklin. According to the young scholar, Franklin was born in Boston, moved to Philadelphia, met a pretty woman who smiled at him, married her—and discovered electricity.

I was struck, at this convention, by the emphasis on ideas that I'm sure would have been unheard-of in merchandising ten or fifteen years ago. The sales managers were reminded by a sales expert that feminine beauty was not so much the effect of cosmetics applied on the outside but of the spirit of the person on the inside. They were also told that the best way to sell any product was to love the prospective customer, be genuinely concerned about her as a person, want to help her improve not only her appearance, but her whole life. It was almost like hearing a sermon!

This concern with ethics runs like a shining thread through many commercial enterprises. The next day—Wednesday—we were in Burlington, Wisconsin, where Norman spoke to employees of a company that makes feed concentrates for livestock. Here again, other speakers emphasized the importance of absolute purity in the manufacture of animal foods, and the importance of honesty and reliability in business methods. I found myself wishing that some of the younger generation who consider businessmen ruthless and soulless moneymaking machines could have listened. They might have learned something!

At this meeting, held in a tent, agricultural exhibits laid out along the sides included a couple of cages containing chickens. During a pause in Norman's speech a jubilant cackling seemed to come through the loudspeaker. Norman was mystified. The audience laughed and so did he when a man opened the cage and held up a newly-laid egg. Chuckling, Norman told the big crowd it was the first time he had ever been interrupted by a chicken and brought the house down with the remark, "Anyway, the hen laid the egg. I didn't."

People sometimes ask Norman and me what we have learned from all our travels. To answer that question properly would take another book, but perhaps I can offer some partial answers.

To begin with, travel makes you grateful for the privilege of being an American. Some of our far-outs decry this country and want to ditch it. But the fact is, even with its faults, it's the best in the world for everyone. No matter how vivid an imagination you may possess, you cannot really begin to be aware of the contrast between our way of life and life in some less fortunate countries until you have actually seen and smelled the poverty and the misery that prevail. When I got to India and was told that 100,000 people slept on the streets of Calcutta every night because they had no home at all, I could not believe it. But I believed it when I saw them lying like bundles of rags on the sidewalks outside our hotel.

Seeing problems in the raw like that also makes you realize that treating symptoms alone isn't enough; you have to attack the root causes. Handing out a bowl of rice to every beggar in Bombay would solve nothing, except to ease their hunger pangs momentarily. You begin to see that it will take new and more fertile strains of rice, new and cheaper and more efficient plows, more education, less illiteracy, more industrialization, and some form of population control, if the situation is ever to be improved.

Travel also makes you realize how deep some of the political divisions in the world really are, and how difficult it is for lasting peace to be obtained. I sometimes think that those who clamor so vociferously here at home for peace and disarmament have no conception of the tremendous forces at work *against* peace in places like the Middle East. It's still a dangerous world that we live in, much as I wish it were otherwise.

Travel also helps us see ourselves as others see us. This is not always a pleasant experience; America is far from being universally loved or admired abroad. The billions of dollars we have handed out have not always been spent in ways that brought us friendship or gratitude. Sometimes I think we Americans should stop trying to make the world over in our own image. There are many places where our ideas and ideals, our values and our standards simply do not work and should not be applied.

I think we are slowly finding this out . . . just as the church in its missionary program had to find it out. For one hundred years the missionary church built compounds, lived inside them isolated from the people, tried to change or destroy the customs of the people among whom they found themselves. The church finally learned to come out of its compounds, respect native customs, give autonomy to native churches. But the change came grudgingly, and almost too late.

I remember once hearing a European say sardonically, "Greece gave us philosophy and architecture. Rome gave us law. The Arabs gave us mathematics. And what does America give us? Coca-Cola—and I like Coca-Cola too!"

I think America has given a lot more than that. It has given blood and treasure on a scale no other nation has ever attempted, much less matched. It has defended nations too weak to defend themselves. But the fact remains that we are not too popular with peoples elsewhere.

One reason, of course, is the behavior of the kind of tourist who has come to be known as the Ugly American. He is loud, vulgar, unattractive and obnoxious—and you see him all too often, throwing his weight around and giving all his fellow-citizens a bad name. I can still hear his strident voice shouting at some shopkeeper or merchant, "Okay, okay, what's that in *real* money?" It makes you want to crawl under the nearest rug.

But there are some great Americans overseas, too. In the military. In the diplomatic corps. In all sorts of commercial jobs. These people are ambassadors of goodwill, and their presence goes a long way toward counteracting the Ugly Americans.

I suppose in the long run the most important lesson that travel teaches is that all nations are made up of human beings who really have many more things in common than barriers between them. The last time we were in Bombay, for instance, Norman gave a talk at the Rotary Club. It was heard by several hundred people, practically all of them Indians. This was publicized in the press and that afternoon our phone rang constantly with calls from people who had read his books and wanted to talk with him.

Since we couldn't see them all separately, we decided to have a sort of informal get-together the next morning at ten o'clock in one of the large parlors of the hotel. At least fifty people came, mostly men. They were industrialists, politicians, civic leaders of every kind. They represented every kind of religion, too. When Norman asked for a show of hands from Christians, only four hands went up, and two of them belonged to us. But as Norman spoke to those in that room—Christian minister talking to Parsees, Hindus, Moslems—a strange thing happened. An awareness somehow came to all of us that where faith is concerned, the needs of everyone are the same, and that above and beyond the differences of religions a universal principle of truth and brotherhood exists. An indescribable feeling of love and unity came into the atmosphere, so strong that it was almost tangible. I felt it. Norman felt it. Everyone felt it. It was a deeply moving moment, one that we'll never forget.

There was an echo of it, too, in New Delhi. Here Norman was approached in the lobby of our hotel by an Indian reporter who wanted an interview. He seemed a very sophisticated and faintly hostile person, and Norman—who is very sensitive to such vibrations—became rather wary. When the man wanted to discuss explosive topics, Norman declined. "I won't talk about political matters," he said to the man. "But I will talk about God."

At once an astonishing change came over the reporter. All the hostility disappeared. "Yes," he said, "I would much prefer to talk about God. I am a seeker—but how do I find

Him? I am not satisfied with my own religion. I wish you would tell me about God."

They had a long and earnest conversation. At the end, to Norman's astonishment, the man knelt down and asked him to put his hands on his head and bless him. Such a thing might be unheard-of in New York, but it is not unusual in India. So Norman put his hands on the reporter's head and said gently, "I bless you in the name of the God who belongs to us all. And since I am a minister of Jesus Christ, I ask in His name that peace and understanding may come into your heart."

Such are the episodes that one would miss if one did not travel. We are fortunate, indeed, to have experienced so many.

❧ 18 ❧

JUST FOR
FUN

A Very Short Play in Two Acts

Cast of characters: WELL-KNOWN PREACHER and WIFE
*Place: Interlaken, Switzerland. A balcony on the
   Hotel Victoria-Jungfrau*
Time: Ten o'clock on a warm summer morning

ACT I

WELL-KNOWN PREACHER (*gazing pensively at the Jungfrau,
   which happens to be obscured by clouds*): "You
   know, I have an idea. But I'd better not tell you what
   it is, because you wouldn't approve."

*Expectant silence. Wife, who is knitting, says
   nothing.*

WELL-KNOWN PREACHER: "Did you hear me? I said I had
   an excellent idea. But I'd better not tell you about it,
   because it would just upset you."

Wife knits on placidly.

WELL-KNOWN PREACHER: "Do you think I ought to tell
   you? Or would you rather remain happy and undis-
   turbed?"

192

WIFE (*calmly*): "Whatever you think best, dear." (*She puts away her knitting.*) "I think the sun is going to come out. Why don't we go for a walk around the meadow?"

WELL-KNOWN PREACHER (*wistfully*): "Don't you want to know what my idea is?"

WIFE: "Certainly. But only when you're ready to tell me. Oh, look, you can see the mountain now. Come on, let's walk."

ACT II

It is thirteen hours later. The well-known preacher and wife are getting ready for bed.

WELL-KNOWN PREACHER: "You know, I think I'd better tell you about that idea I had after all. It will upset you, because it involves changing plans, and I know how you hate changing plans once they're made. But I've been thinking. Instead of going to Hamburg as our itinerary calls for, and shipping the car home from there with all that bother and red tape, why don't we drive it back to Stuttgart where we got it and let the Mercedes people worry about shipping the car? We could fly home from there. It really makes a lot more sense, don't you think?"

WIFE (*cheerfully*): "Yes, I do."

WELL-KNOWN PREACHER (*incredulously*): "You mean, you're not upset?"

WIFE: "Why, no. Not at all."

WELL-KNOWN PREACHER: "Well, that's fine. I was afraid you would be. Are you *sure* you're not?"

WIFE: "Quite sure."

WELL-KNOWN PREACHER: "Well, that's great. Because if you had been upset, then I'd have been upset. It's all settled then. We'll go to Stuttgart, not Hamburg, right?"

WIFE: "Right."

They climb into bed, switch out the lights. Silence. But not for long.

WELL-KNOWN PREACHER: "Ruth, are you sure this change of plans doesn't bother you?"

WIFE: "Quite sure."

WELL-KNOWN PREACHER: "Positive?"

WIFE: "Positive!"

Long pause.

WELL-KNOWN PREACHER: "But *why* aren't you upset?"

WIFE: "Well, dear, I don't want to depress you, but that idea wasn't exactly new."

WELL-KNOWN PREACHER: "It wasn't?"

WIFE: "No, it wasn't. It's exactly what I suggested to you three weeks ago in New York."

WELL-KNOWN PREACHER (*weakly*): "You did?"

WIFE: "Yes, I did. We were sitting in the kitchen at the Hill Farm, and we were planning this trip, and I said we ought to have the car shipped home from Stuttgart and then fly from there. But you said you wanted to go to Hamburg."

WELL-KNOWN PREACHER (*amazed*): "I did?"

WIFE: "Yes, you did. Don't you remember?"

WELL-KNOWN PREACHER: "Well, now that you mention it, I do seem to recall some sort of discussion along those lines."

WIFE: "It's still a good idea. There's nothing wrong with having it twice."

Silence. Finally . . .

WIFE: "Good night, dear."

WELL-KNOWN PREACHER (*in small voice*): "Good night."

🌿 19 🌿

SUNDAY AT
THE
WHITE HOUSE

🌿 To me, one of the most fascinating places in the world is the home of our presidents, the White House in Washington, D.C. It's not large compared to some presidential mansions or royal palaces. But it offers a unique combination of stateliness, history, beauty, and charm—plus a kind of warm livability that makes it the ultimate in the American home. Norman and I have been fortunate enough to be entertained there several times, and so many people have asked me what it was like that in this chapter I shall try to describe one of those visits.

The one I have in mind took place on June 15, 1969, a Sunday which also happened to be Father's Day. It was the first time Norman preached at the White House; he was there again some six months later. But I remember that first occasion vividly, because we also had the privilege of lunching privately with President Nixon and all of his family.

It began with an unexpected telephone call from Washington. "This is the White House calling. Is Dr. Peale there?" As it happened, Dr. Peale was *not* there, so the call came to me. At the other end of the line was one of the President's assistants, Bud Wilkinson, the famous former football coach. He spoke of the plan the President had inaugurated of

196

having Sunday morning services at the White House to which about three hundred and fifty people were invited. The President would be pleased if Norman would conduct the service on Father's Day. If we could come to Washington the night before, Mr. Wilkinson said, he would arrange to have our plane met. The next day, another White House car would bring us to the Executive Mansion in time for the service, which was scheduled for eleven o'clock. Mr. Wilkinson hoped that I would let him know as soon as possible whether or not Norman, who was out of the city on a speaking engagement, would be able to accept. I assured him that I would.

Actually, Norman had mixed feelings about the invitation. He knew, of course, that it was a great honor, and he wanted to do anything to please the President, whom he had known for more than a quarter of a century and whom he admired greatly. But he also felt a strong sense of obligation to his own church and his own congregation. Would some people think he was more interested in the glamor and publicity of a White House appearance than in doing the regular job he was supposed to do?

We discussed it at length, and felt that a Presidential invitation, rather like a royal command, was a great opportunity to be of possible spiritual help. With all his problems and responsibilities, the President probably needed a lift more than anyone!

Accordingly, when Norman began to shape his sermon he built it around problems and the part they play in human lives.

We flew to Washington on Saturday afternoon and were met, as promised, by a Presidential aide and driven to the Madison Hotel. Promptly at ten-thirty the next morning, another car and another aide picked us up and drove us to the White House. Guards at the gate checked our credentials and waved us through. At the entrance to the mansion yet another aide, resplendent in military uniform, greeted us and asked if Norman would like to see the room where he would be preaching. This turned out to be the East Room, the largest room in the White House, impressive with its gleaming floor, gold and ivory draperies, and portraits of George and Martha Washington. Chairs had been set up in the room under the great crystal chandeliers, and a microphone. Two chairs were placed behind the microphone, evidently for the President and Norman. There was no altar. The service was to be simple and nondenominational: an invocation, a hymn, a selection by a choir, the sermon, and a closing prayer. It would last only about half an hour.

We were then taken upstairs to a private sitting room in the Presidential family's part of the mansion. It was handsomely decorated in yellow and gold, with cabinets around the wall containing exquisite art objects and gifts received by many Presidents. Here we joined the President and Mrs. Nixon, their daughter Julie and David Eisenhower (whom Norman had married the previous December), their other daughter Tricia, and the recently appointed Chief Justice Warren Burger and his wife, whom we had not met before.

Pat Nixon was wearing a lovely blue summer suit with matching scarf at her throat. They greeted us warmly and offered us coffee and small Danish pastries. The President asked how things were at the Marble Church and said he missed the services there. He also told us that his daughters had given him a surfboard for Father's Day and had dared him to try it when he got back to California. I told Mrs. Nixon that I had been following her travels in the newspapers, and everyone made small talk until a few minutes before eleven, when an aide came in to escort Justice and Mrs. Burger and the young Eisenhowers and Tricia to the East Room.

Apparently, up to this point, it had been the custom for the President's wife and the wife of the visiting minister to go to the service together, leaving the President and the minister to arrive a few moments later. But now Pat Nixon said to me, "Ruth, we've always been in the habit of going to church with our husbands, so why not in the White House, too? You go with Norman, and I'll go with the President." (She always refers to her husband as "the President" as does everyone else; first names disappear at that level, no matter how long or intimate a friendship may be.) So the four of us went downstairs paired off as she suggested.

When we came into the East Room, everyone stood up as a mark of respect to the President. Seats were reserved for us in front. I sat with Julie Eisenhower on my left. Mrs. Nixon was on my right, with an empty chair on the aisle where the President would sit after he had introduced Norman.

The service began with an invocation by Norman, designed, I knew, to bring a feeling of peace and tranquility to this, the nerve center of a troubled nation:

Almighty God, our Heavenly Father, help everyone here this day to sense Thy presence. May the world, with all of its confusion and its demands, retreat for these moments, and may we be with Thee in the peace of eternity. "Thou wilt keep him in perfect peace, whose mind is stayed on thee." "Come unto me, all ye that labour and are heavy laden, and I will give you rest." "Peace I give unto you: not as the world giveth, give I unto you. Let not your heart be troubled, neither let it be afraid." We invoke Thy divine blessing upon this service, upon this house, upon the President of the United States and his family and all those who with him are charged with the government of this blessed land. God bless America and all of its people. Bring peace in our time, O Lord. May all of the children of men have a new sense of Thy guidance. Through Jesus Christ our Lord. Amen.

The simple service proceeded swiftly. A Black choir sang softly and beautifully. Finally the President stood up and introduced Norman, and I felt a deep glow of pride in my husband at his warm and friendly words: "Since we first met Dr. Peale twenty-five years ago at the end of World War II," the President said, "we have had the opportunity, my wife and I, and later our daughters, to hear him on many occasions. During the years that we lived in New York we not only knew him from his sermons, but had the privilege of knowing him personally and knowing Mrs. Peale as well and their family. And I can say that never have we heard him over those many times that he has not been a great inspiration to us. This house is privileged to have conducting our worship service this morning, Dr. Norman Vincent Peale."

Norman then delivered the sermon, which was tape-recorded. He spoke as he always does, spontaneously and without notes. Since it has never appeared anywhere else, I thought you might like to read his remarks. Here is what Norman said that sultry day in June to the assembled White House guests:

Mr. President, Mrs. Nixon, David, Julie, Tricia, and friends all:

It is indeed an honor to be here this morning to conduct a service of worship at the invitation of the President of the United States. I must say that we miss the President and Mrs. Nixon in New York, particularly at the Marble Collegiate Church, where they attended so many times in the years gone by. And I will have to admit publicly that he is the one and only member of my congregation whom I helped to move to another city. It is also a privilege to see again one of the most wonderful young couples I ever had the pleasure of uniting in matrimony, and also their lovely sister Patricia.

This is Father's Day, when we honor our fathers and express our love for them. It's a privilege to preach in the presence of the first father of the nation. I don't know whether he's ever been called that before or not, but this is what he is—father to his children, and in a deep sense, presiding from this historic and venerated place, the father of his people.

Being a father myself, I know something about the problems that a father possesses; and I wish to speak to you for just a few moments on that phenomenon known as a problem. I think people generally take a dim view of it. They assume that there is something inherently bad about a problem. And they believe that life would be simply wonderful if either they had fewer problems or easier problems or, better still, no problems whatsoever.

Now, actually, would we be better off with fewer or easier or no problems at all? And is a problem inherently a bad thing? May it not, on the contrary, be a very good thing? Let me answer my own question by telling you of an incident.

I was walking down Fifth Avenue in New York City not long ago when I saw approaching me a friend of mine by the name of George. It was obvious from George's disconsolate and melancholy demeanor that he wasn't what you might call filled to overflowing with the ecstasy and exuberance of human existence. Which is a rather fanciful way of saying that he was really dragging bottom; he was low. This excited my natural sympathy; so I asked him, "How are you, George?" Well now, when you get right down to it, that was nothing but a routine inquiry. But George took it seriously and for fifteen minutes he enlightened me meticulously on how bad he felt. And the more he talked, the worse I felt. Finally I said, "Well, George, what seems to be the difficulty?"

This really set him off. "Oh," he said, "it's these problems. Problems, nothing but problems, I am fed up with problems." And he got so exercised about the matter that he quite forgot whom he was talking to, and he began to castigate these problems vitriolically, using in the process thereof, I am sad to relate, a great many theological terms—though he didn't put them together in a theological manner, I assure you. But I knew what he meant all right, for he had what the super-erudite call the "power to communicate."

"Well," I said, "George, I certainly would like to help you if I can. What can I do for you?"

"Oh," he said, "get me rid of these problems."

I said, "Do you mean that? All of them?"

"Yes," he said, "all of them."

Well, always being willing to oblige as best I can, I said, "George, the other day I was up in the northern part of New York City in the Bronx on professional business in a place where the head man told me there were some 150,000 people and not a single one of them had a problem."

The first enthusiasm I saw in George flashed up in his eyes and suffused his countenance as he said, "Boy, that's for me! Lead me to this place."

I said, "All right, you asked for it. It's Woodlawn Cemetery in the Bronx." And this is a fact: Nobody in Woodlawn has a problem. They couldn't care less what we will see on television tonight or read in tomorrow morning's newspapers. They have no problems at all. But—they are dead.

It therefore follows, I believe, in logical sequence, that problems constitute a sign of life. Indeed, I would go so far as to say that the more problems you have, the more alive you are. The man who has, let's say, ten good old tough, man-sized problems is twice as alive as the poor, miserable, apathetic character who only has five problems.

Problems are written into the constitution of the universe. When God made this universe the way it is, He inserted into it the phenomenon of a problem. For what purpose? Well, I can only guess at what was in His mind, but what I know about Him would indicate that what He wants to do is to make real people out of us. For you never grow strong without resistance and struggle; and problems are part of that phenomenon known as struggle. So I call to your attention on this Father's Day the idea that problems are good for individuals and for a great developing, evolving nation. As the nation solves its problems, it will produce a strong people.

What, then, are a few suggestions for handling a problem? There's a text in Philippians—4:13—which comes to mind, "I can do all things through Christ which strengtheneth me." One of the modern interpretations of that passage is this: "I have the strength to face all conditions by the power that Christ gives me." With that as a background, I suggest three principles for handling a problem: First, the *in-spite-of* principle; second, the *relentless-pressure* principle; and, third, the *as-if* principle.

What do we mean by the *in-spite-of* principle? It means that when you are fortified by an inward consciousness of God and the Lord Jesus Christ you look at your problems and you say, "Yes, I see you. You are very formidable, you are very complicated, but in spite of what you are, I have what it takes to handle you." And we do, too—if we trust God and if we think. And the two are one and inseparable, because real trust in God is the profoundest thinking known to man.

I have a humble little illustration about a boy fifteen years old. He was an unusual boy. The summer vacation came along, and he said to his father, "Dad, I don't want to sponge on you all summer. I want a job." The father, when he recovered from his surprise, encouraged him in this. So he read the want ads, and found a job offer which said that applicants should show up the next morning at eight o'clock. He was there. But so were twenty other boys, lined up facing the secretary of the man doing the hiring.

The average boy might have looked at these other kids and said, "They're all good boys. Any one of them will get the job. I at least tried. I've done the best I can and at the twenty-first position in line there's no opportunity whatsoever . . ." But this boy believed in the *in-spite-of* principle. So he thought, really thought. And if you really think you can get a solution to any problem that will ever face you.

An inspiration came to him. He took a piece of paper; he wrote something quickly on it. He walked over to the secretary of the man doing the hiring, a rather formidable-looking girl. He bowed politely to her and said, "Miss, this message is of the utmost importance to your boss. Please deliver it to him immediately."

She looked at the message and she smiled. She immediately rose, went into the office, laid the message on the desk of the boss, who read it—and laughed out loud, for this is what it said: "Dear Sir: I am the twenty-first kid in line. Don't do anything until you see me." It would seem that all of us who are believers in God and His sustaining power and guidance should know that we, like that young man, have the inner capacity to handle any problem.

He made use of the *in-spite-of* principle. That's one great formula for solving problems.

The second is the *relentless-pressure* principle. Obviously, I have to give these very sketchily because of the limitations of time, but it's a simple thing. Nobody ever succeeded at anything in this life who didn't keep everlastingly at it. If it won't respond one way, you come at it another way. You attack it from before and behind, from above and below, any way that there's the slightest opportunity to gain the objective and the result. If you "can do all things through Christ" who gives you the strength, then if your goal and objective are right, reached in prayer and meditation and under the guidance of God, you have just got to keep at it until you gain a victory.

Not long ago, I visited at Chartwell in Kent, Churchill's old home. While I was there, somebody told me about the time Churchill was invited by the headmaster of Harrow School to come and give a talk. At one time he had been a student there. The headmaster told the boys that an immortal utterance was going to be made, one that they'd remember until their dying days, and he had them properly conditioned for it. At the appointed time, the great man came. He stood before them; he pulled his glasses down over his nose, as was his custom, and looked them over—bright young boyish faces—and he went back into the long reaches of memory to when a little boy sat out there in one of those same benches in which students have carved their initials for six hundred years. And he saw this little fellow who was shy and who stuttered. He had great thoughts even then, but the words piled up under his tongue. Yet, in time, he spoke and wrote the greatest English of our era. And a dead silence fell. Finally he spoke this immortal message: "Never give in, *never, never, never, never.*" That was the essence of his speech. And a great, profound philosophical truth had been uttered—the *relentless-pressure* principle.

"I have the strength to face all conditions . . ." I believe this, friends. I am positive of it! "I have the strength to face all conditions . . ." Through my own strength and wisdom? Why, of course not. But "by the power that Christ gives me."

And principle number three is the *as-if* principle. This principle was first announced by the late professor William James, who at one time taught, so I understand, anatomy, philosophy, and psychology at Harvard—which meant, you might say, that he was professor of body, mind, and soul. He was the father of American philosophical psychology, one of the great men of our history. He announced the *as-if* principle. It means that if you have one condition, and you're dissatisfied with it, and you want another which is greater, you act *as if* you had the other—and all the forces of your nature conspire to produce this condition in fact. If you are full of fear, for example, and anxiety, and you want to be full of courage and confidence, you try—feebly at first, but you try—to act as if you had those virtues. And something in the construction of our nature brings it realistically into being.

There are lots of people who have problems. I have a letter here from a little girl. Naturally, I'll not give you her name nor tell where she lives, but just say she's a very young girl. This is her letter: "Dear Dr. Peale, I have this problem that I would like you to send me some booklets on. My mother is on dope, and I am living with my grandmother. My mother never married. We don't get to see her very often, that's my sister and I. And could you put her on your prayer list? I go to church every Sunday. I'm only nine years old, so I don't really understand."

All the pathos of human life is in this plea of a little girl for a better life. She wants me to pray for her mother. She wants to know how she can overcome these problems. What did I write her? I told her how deeply I felt her problems and how proud I was of her strength in facing up to them. Then I wrote, "Honey, you just try to get even more acquainted with Jesus Christ, because He will help you to handle any condition." And I described as best I could to her the *as-if* principle: "Just act as if you're going to have a good life, and I can assure you that you will."

Prayer: Our Heavenly Father, bless this message to our hearts and help us to live with Thee and with Thy Son Jesus Christ so faithfully that strength and power and peace and goodness will fill our hearts forever. Through Jesus Christ our Lord. Amen.

Go in peace, and may the peace of God go with you.

When the service ended, the President and Norman left the East Room together. Then Mrs. Nixon and I followed. The other guests waited while photographers took some pictures of the four of us as a memento of the occasion. And then the entire Nixon family joined us for pictures. After this we went into the State Dining Room with its gold draperies and light green walls and formed a receiving line under the portrait of Abraham Lincoln.

The guests filed by, and standing with the President and Mrs. Nixon, we shook hands with all of them. I remember being impressed with the diversity of the people—there were cabinet members and senators, but also people from the White House staff, chauffeurs, maids, telephone operators. Some came as families, complete with children. One very old gentleman told the President how he had met Theodore Roosevelt on that very spot sixty-five years ago. "What do you remember best about him?" the President wanted to know. "The beautiful striped trousers he wore!" said the old gentleman promptly. President Nixon looked down at his own dark suit and smiled. "Times have changed," he said dryly.

The thing that impressed me most was the way the President seemed to give his complete attention to the person he was greeting. He knew practically everyone's name, and his observations to each guest were quick and humorous. After they had passed through the receiving line, the guests found little cakes and coffee set out on the long table where so many of the world's crowned heads and chiefs of state have been entertained since 1817 when the White House, burned by the British during the War of 1812, was finally restored during President Monroe's term of office.

When the reception was over, we took an elevator to the family floor, where Mrs. Nixon showed us various rooms. One of them in Lincoln's time had been the room where the cabinet met. Another was a small room with a fireplace, where, during the Civil War, telegrams came in from the battlefronts. It gave me a feeling almost of awe to think of Abe Lincoln standing in that room, tall and gaunt, probably often in his nightshirt, receiving reports of apparently endless setbacks and defeats, but never losing his courage or his faith that ultimately the Union would be preserved.

There was an old armchair in the room near the fireplace. Mrs. Nixon told us that that chair had belonged to her husband since his earliest days in law practice, and had been with him through all the ups and downs of his political career. I felt sure that the placing of the chair in that spot was no accident. It would be only natural, when the terrible pressures of his office weighed heavily, for this twentieth-century President to sit in his old chair in this room and draw strength and encouragement from the memory of his great predecessor.

Mrs. Nixon told us that Mrs. John Eisenhower, Julie's mother-in-law, and Susan Eisenhower, David's sister, were to join us for luncheon. We waited for them in one of the areas of the long wide hallway that runs through the upper floor of the White House, each with its little grouping of furniture, tasteful and restful. As we sat there I noticed in each ashtray a little paper book of matches, white with gold lettering that said, "The President's House." I asked if I might have one for a souvenir. "Certainly," said my hostess, "take three or four and give them to your children."

Luncheon in the small private dining room was a simple affair. At the President's request, Norman said grace. The meal consisted of fruit cup, green salad, creamed chicken, peas, and ice cream. Two waiters served us deftly and unobtrusively. I remember I asked Pat Nixon if she had to worry about such things as menus. "Oh, no," she said cheerfully, "I never know at family dinners what we're going to have until I sit down at the table." I was inclined to envy her this happy state of affairs. Genuineness and simplicity marked this happy First Family. Indeed, Mrs. Nixon was living out beautifully the adventure of being a wife.

By now it had begun to rain outside, and the President— who loves open fires—ordered the fire lighted. The flames crackled merrily, and so did the conversation. The President talked freely about national and world affairs, and everyone joined in, even the young people who had strong-minded views and did not hesitate to express them forthrightly.

Sitting on the President's right, I told him about our

summer plans for a trip around the world. He looked thoughtful for a moment. "Norman," he said finally, "I have a job for you."

Norman told me later that he could not imagine what his host had in mind. But he said that he would be happy to do anything that the President wanted.

"If you're going around the world," the President continued, "I'd like you to stop in Viet Nam, go among our troops, and visit some of our wounded in the hospitals there. I'd like you to talk to them just the way you talk to your congregation at the Marble Church, give them a lift, let them know that people back home appreciate the sacrifices they're making. I think that if you'd do it, you'd be making a real contribution. We'll set the whole thing up for you in advance. What do you say?"

Norman said that he would be glad to do what he could, and my practical mind immediately went to work revising schedules and altering plans. I knew that Norman had been anxious to go overseas as a chaplain in World War II, that his friends and advisers had talked him out of it on the grounds that he would be more useful and come into contact with more servicemen and women if he stayed in his own pulpit. So I thought he would find this chance to go into a combat zone, and be of some help to the men there, stimulating and exciting.

And this, indeed, was the way it all turned out.

After luncheon, the President offered to show us some of the other rooms of the White House. We protested that he had spent too much time with us already, but he insisted, and I must say it was remarkable how unhurried and unpressured he managed to seem. Looking at the marvelous furniture and the magnificent portraits of so many national heroes—Franklin, Jefferson, Daniel Webster, and many others—I thought of all the history this marvelous old house had seen since the days when Abigail Adams, wife of the second President, used to dry her laundry in the then vacant and unfurnished East Room. I wished that every American could see it as we were seeing it—and indeed I believe about a million Americans a year do have the privilege of seeing some of it, although not with such distinguished guides!

The President finally took us into his famed oval office. Here he presented Norman with a golf ball with the President's name stamped on it. By now the rain was coming down heavily, and our car was supposed to be waiting for us. Actually, the car was a bit late, and we all stood at the entrance waiting for it. Again we urged our host to leave us, but he refused. When the car did come, he thanked us both again for coming and Norman for conducting the service.

Driving away, we looked back at the grand old mansion standing there in the silver rain. "It makes you feel proud, doesn't it?" Norman said suddenly. "To be a part of something like that. To be an American. To know that such a magnificent heritage is ours."

"Yes," I said, and I meant it. "Very proud."

🌿 20 🌿

HOW TO
BEND A TWIG

🌿 There's only one place where character can be built.

In the home.

In our home, when the youngsters were growing up, we found that certain principles seemed to be effective when it came to getting the results we wanted. Here, then, are a few homemade hints for parents on how to bend a twig.

1. BE THERE

One Sunday some years ago, after Norman had preached his second sermon of the morning, a man who had been in the congregation asked if he could speak with us. He looked like what he said he was: a successful salesman. He was, in fact, the star salesman for a company in New Jersey that made electronic devices—tape recorders, record players, and so on. His problem, it seemed, had to do with his teen-age son. After hearing Norman's sermon, which dealt with family problems, he had decided to ask for advice.

The boy, he said, was an introvert. He lacked determination, self-confidence, drive. He didn't seem interested in school activities. All he liked to do, apparently, was stay by himself and read. "I just don't understand it," the man said. "When I was his age, I was ready to try anything. Even today, the success I've had depends on energy, outgoingness, willingness to hustle. Believe me, it's frustrating when your only son seems to be so deficient in the characteristics that are essential for success in life."

Since Norman had asked me to sit in on the discussion, I asked the man what his wife did. "Oh," he said, "she's like me. She's a real dynamo, lots of outside interests, always involved in some sort of civic work."

Norman and I exchanged glances: We had encountered cases like this before. "Mr. So-and-so," Norman said, "how much time do you spend with your boy?"

The man seemed taken aback. "Spend with him? Well, I see him every day, at breakfast. Except when I'm on the road, naturally."

"I know that," Norman said. "But do you ever roughhouse with him, or offer to play catch, or go to a movie with him, or take him fishing or hunting?"

"Well, no," the man said. "There doesn't seem to be time . . . "

"Do you and his mother," Norman continued, "ever go to watch him in any kind of school activity? Do you ever sit with him at a school basketball game or a football game or a track meet?"

"Well, no," the man said again. "But, as I told you, he doesn't seem to get involved in school activities."

"Mr. So-and-so," Norman said, "it's not often that I can diagnose a problem in human relations in five minutes and offer an almost certain cure, but this time I think I can. The prescription is simple, and it consists of just two words: *Be there.* Reorganize your busy life so that you have some time for your son. Which is more important: Making one more sale, or giving back to your boy the self-confidence that obviously he has lost? Why is he so timid, so retiring? It's because he doesn't have the backing that every child needs, the feeling that his parents are there when he needs them, showing interest, giving encouragement, caring about what happns to him. *Be there*. Write those words on a label and paste them on your shaving mirror, in your hat, on your desk, in your briefcase. Put them where you'll see them twenty times a day. Put them where your wife will see them too. Don't expect miracles, because it's obvious that you have let this situation go on much too long. But I can guarantee that if you do what I'm suggesting, a year from now you'll see a miraculous change in your boy."

Exactly fifty-two Sundays later the man was back with his wife and his son. "I just wanted you to meet Donny," he said. "He's a junior in high school now. He plays second-string football and basketball, he recently had a part in the school play, and just the other day he was elected vice-president of his class!" He put his hand on the boy's shoulder. "You don't know how proud I am of this young man. Or how grateful I am to you."

Norman smiled at him. "Keep that sign on your shaving mirror," he said.

"Don't worry," the man said. "It's the most effective two-word rule I know!"

We always considered it so in our house. From the time our own youngsters were very small, Norman and I were aware that unless we were very careful, our crowded schedules outside the home might become a menace to our children. And so we made a special effort to "be there" when it mattered. If one of us had to go on a trip, the other stayed home. If a child was involved in a kindergarten play, a Sunday School pageant, a high school debate, an athletic event, anything where parental support and encouragement were needed, we made it an ironclad rule to be on hand.

Once, I remember, John had an important role in a Gilbert & Sullivan production at his school, Deerfield Academy in Massachusetts. A couple of days before the performance, he called us in a panic. He was sure he couldn't do it; his voice would fail him at the last minute; he would forget his lines, and so on. We had planned to go up to the school the day of the performance. But it was obvious that John needed support sooner than that. We canceled about a dozen engagements and went up to Deerfield the day before the show. We didn't make a great thing of it. We were simply *there*. We let John know that we were sure he would do a fine job. Norman told him that everyone had stage fright; that after preaching hundreds of sermons and making scores of speeches he still had butterflies every time himself. The result was predictable: John stayed nervous, but not panicky—and when the time came he sang and acted splendidly.

I remember another occasion when Margaret had a part in a play put on by the children at the Marble Church. We went and sat with the other parents. Later she told me of looking out into the audience when the lights were dimmed.

"Almost all the faces were in shadow," she said. "But you and Daddy were sitting in a faint patch of light. Every time I looked out across the footlights into the darkness, I could see both your faces. It gave me a wonderful, warm feeling inside. . . ."

A warm, wonderful feeling inside. . . . The best way to give it to your children is to be there. It's the best investment a parent can make.

2.   TEACH THEM TO STAND UP FOR THEIR RIGHTS

Children, like the rest of us, sometimes allow themselves to be taken advantage of because the ethics they've been taught usually stress tolerance and forbearance even in the face of considerable provocation. But, clearly, there's a point where self-defense becomes justifiable. As someone said, "Your right to swing your fist ends at the point where my nose begins." I think part of a parent's job is to help his child understand this.

Ministers' children, in particular, hear so much about the Golden Rule and the virtue in "turning the other cheek" that quite often they don't know where to draw the line. I remember very well the day John came home from school —he was about seven—and told his father that he no longer liked Harold, one of his classmates.

"Why?" asked Norman. "What did Harold do?"

"He said he was going to spit on my tie!"

"And did he spit on your tie?"

"Yes, he did!"

"Did you tell him to stop?"

"Yes, but he said he would do it again. And he will, too."

"Well," said Norman, "if he does it again, I'd take a punch at him, if I were you."

"You would?" asked John incredulously.

"Yes, I would!" said Norman forthrightly.

Sure enough, Harold did spit on John's tie; John did take a punch at him; Harold took the hint and stopped spitting, and the two became the best of friends.

The moral is plain: Don't retreat past the line where you give in to bullying or lose your self-respect. This is an important lesson for any child to learn, because he'll be needing it for the rest of his life.

3. Go Along With Their Harmless Hang-ups

Quite often children will have strong feelings about some things that seem rather foolish from an adult point of view but are completely valid to them. Our philosophy was always to take a tolerant view and make whatever adjustments were necessary—so long as no one was seriously inconvenienced, or family standards noticeably lowered.

There was the time, for example, when our three youngsters announced that they didn't want to go to Sunday

School any more; they would rather go to church. We talked it over and decided that church attendance was a reasonable substitute for Sunday School attendance—provided I read them the Bible and gave them equivalent instructions at home, which I was willing to do.

This worked well for a time. Then they informed us that they were not happy about going to church, either. This called for some intensive discussion. When we probed into the problem, we found that the thing that bothered them was sitting in the minister's pew. As in many churches, the pastor's pew at Marble Collegiate Church is a bit special, with a silver plaque which says "Pastors." "When we sit there," Margaret said glumly, "everybody knows our father is the minister."

It was being conspicuous that was troubling them, not church attendance as such. "If that's all it is," we said to them, "you can sit anywhere you like, and be as anonymous as you please."

Delighted with this solution, all three of them chose widely separated seats in the balcony and they kept this up for several years. Actually, they were more conspicuous than before, because the congregation soon spotted them. Quite often, before starting his sermon, Norman would look up and smile at each of them, and people would watch for this little family game that gave a personal touch to the service.

Eventually, as they grew older, they all came back to the pastor's pew. I always sat on the end as Norman preached, with the children on the inside. But one day when he was about sixteen, John gravely motioned to me to change places with him, which I did. No one said anything, but the gesture was unmistakable. Unless his father could be there, he was telling us, *he* was the man of the family now.

It's fascinating—and a little poignant, too—for the mother

of a son to watch him move gradually away from her protective and maternal shelter and into his father's masculine orbit. One night, I remember, when John was about fifteen, he came home quite late from a party. Norman had gone to bed; I was still up. For some reason, John was full of talk . . . so we talked on and on about all sorts of things. Suddenly, at about two in the morning, John said abruptly, "Where's my father? I ought to be talking to him about these things. Where's Dad?"

Dad was sound asleep, but something in John sounded so serious and so urgent that—putting aside my faintly wounded pride—I went in and woke Norman out of a sound sleep. I told him that John wanted to talk to him.

"What's wrong?" said Norman, looking dazedly at the clock.

"Nothing's wrong," I said. "Your son just wants to talk to you, that's all."

"At this hour?" cried my poor husband. "Can't he wait until morning?"

"I don't think so," I said. "I have a feeling you should talk to him now."

So Norman floundered into bathrobe and slippers and went into the living room where John was waiting. Discreetly, I left them alone. They talked—man-to-man, for a couple of hours. Later, Norman thanked me for waking him; he said it was the first conversation he had ever had with John where they seemed to be two individuals exchanging ideas, rather than a father and son communicating with difficulty across the generation gap.

4. WHEN IN DOUBT—TRUST

On a recent trip out West, Norman and I met a married couple who introduced us to their teen-age daughter. She was a quiet, well-mannered girl, but somehow over-docile, spiritless. Later, when the daughter was not with us, the mother began to voice the fears she had about the temptations and pitfalls that she believed surrounded her child. All the children in the local high school, she said, were exposed to drug abuse. Sex immorality was rampant. She and her husband imposed strict curfews on the girl; they had to know exactly where she was at every moment. The mother ended by saying that she was not going to let her daughter go away to college. There were too many dreadful and corrupting influences on campus nowadays. The girl would be better off at home.

She went on and on, and it seemed to be one of the saddest recitals I had ever heard. The woman did not trust her own child. And because of her lack of trust, she was creating a situation in which ultimately resentment and rebellion could easily bring about some or all of the things she feared most.

It seems to me that if you're a parent, you've *got* to trust your children and let them know that you do. Nothing is so effective in the long run in deterring them from the kind of behavior that may hurt them. A child enclosed by an iron curtain of harsh rules is going to break through that barrier sooner or later. A child surrounded by loving trust is far less likely to betray it.

There are many ways of letting your children know that you trust them. When ours were growing up, we used to stretch their imaginations (and their knowledge of life) by discussing with them problems that were brought to Norman by troubled people. We never used names, but always the situations we discussed were true-life ones. Should the girl pregnant out of wedlock give up her baby for adoption or try to keep it? Was it fair for a boy to be exempt from the draft just because he was in college? We made it clear to the children that there should never be any discussion of such matters outside our home. We trusted them not to gossip about these cases. And they never did.

We trusted their judgment and good sense about the things they read, too. There was never any censorship; they could read any book or magazine in the house. I suppose they could have found undesirable reading material outside the home if they had so desired. But the fact that we trusted them not to abuse the freedom they had was, I think, the main reason why they never did.

Norman has been a guest on the Art Linkletter show on several occasions. Art is a good friend of ours. On one occasion the discussion turned on this matter of trusting children in college. Norman said our daughter Elizabeth was then a student at Mt. Holyoke and that he had unqualified trust in her under any circumstances. He forgot all about this remark. But later when the show was aired it was heard by many Mt. Holyoke students, including Elizabeth. On our next trip to the college, girl after girl came to Norman saying, "You're right, Dr. Peale, Elizabeth is trustworthy. She'll never let you down, never."

So trust your children. Until they prove conclusively that they are untrustworthy, trust them. Trust stimulates response in kind.

5. Don't Let Them Push You Around

Sometimes children react to discipline with anger and resistance. They may fight the embattled parent so fiercely that it's almost frightening. But it's important not to give in if you know you're right.

Once, I remember, when John was fourteen or fifteen he was asked to an evening party at the house of some people who lived in another section of New York. John and I agreed that I would pick him up at eleven-thirty.

Norman was out of the city, so I drove over alone at the appointed time. When I arrived, the party was anything but ended. On the contrary, as sometimes happens with that age group, a kind of mass hysteria had taken over. The boys and girls were running wild, laughing, shouting, wrestling, urging one another on to ever-noisier and more spectacular exploits. The hosts seemed unwilling or unable to control the guests; in fact I had the impression they had not been there all the time.

With some difficulty I located John, as wild-eyed and overexcited as the rest, and told him that it was time to go home. He pointed out with enthusiasm that the party was just warming up, that the real fun had just started, and that it was too early to go home.

I replied that he had been invited for a certain length of time, that it was now time to leave, and that he was coming home with me as planned. He insisted that no one else was going home. If he went home simply because his mother said so, he would be known forever as a mama's boy. His reputation would be ruined.

I repeated, as quietly but also as firmly as I could, that he *was* leaving, whether he liked it or not. I didn't voice my real fear, which was that someone might be injured if the party grew any more uproarious—as I was quite sure it would. I simply told him that it was good manners to leave a party at the indicated time, that we expected our guests to behave in this manner, and that was the way we behaved when we were guests.

He went into an absolute tailspin; I had never seen our normally amiable John in such a fury. But I stuck to my guns. The result was that I shortly found myself driving home with a boy almost hysterical with frustration and resentment. All the way home, choking back tears of rage, he kept repeating that I had made him look ridiculous in front of his friends by treating him like a baby. Why did

I have to be so mean, so hateful? Why couldn't I be under-standing like other parents?

I took refuge in silence, and kept telling myself that I had done the right thing. But long after he had gone to bed, slamming his door in one last futile gesture of defiance, I lay awake wondering if I had alienated my only son in a way that might have permanent consequences. Had I, per-haps, been too rigid, too unyielding? Was this sort of dis-cipline worth it? Even if it all simmered down, might there not be psychic scars that would haunt us both for a long time to come?

The next day neither John nor I mentioned the storm of the night before. But my doubts persisted. Had he really decided to overlook our clash of wills, or was he hiding some deep, unspoken resentment? I told myself that I might never know—and I thought I never would.

But years later, when John was married and had children of his own, I happened to be visiting and somehow the topic of parental discipline came up. "You know, mother," John said reminiscently, "I think you and Dad did a pretty good job with us kids. Not too strict. Not too permissive. Just about right."

Back into my mind flashed the memory of that harrowing night. "I'm sure you didn't think so," I said dryly, "the night I dragged you home from that party at the Bennetts' house and we had such a battle about it."

John looked at me in wonderment. "What party at the Bennetts' house?"

He had completely forgotten the whole episode. Nor did my description of it arouse the faintest flicker of recollec-tion. It was as if the whole thing had never happened.

The message for parents, I think, is plain: Don't let your-self be bullied or blackmailed into giving in to your children just because they seem to resent the enforcement of fair and just discipline. You're their protector. You not only have better judgment than they do; you have the duty and the responsibility to use it—*in their behalf*. If I had given in to John that night, something might have happened that he would *not* have forgotten and might have colored his whole life.

So love your children. Trust them. Be honest with them. Talk to them. Listen to them. Pray for them. Be with them as much as you can. Give them a framework of discipline and security inside which they can grow into strong, self-confident human beings.

Having children, helping them grow, pointing them in the right direction, praising them when they succeed, rescuing them when they fail—all this adds up to a great responsibility. But nothing is more satisfying and rewarding in the great adventure of being a wife.

🌿 21 🌿

RELIGION—
DON'T ANALYZE IT
—LIVE IT

🌿 The other day I was at a meeting with a group of high church denominational officials. Discussion and wrangling had gone on for hours about certain doctrinal matters. As a matter of fact, the discussion centered around the question of whether or not, in this particular denomination, women should be ordained. Finally one young minister said something that struck a chord with everyone. "Wouldn't it be nice," he said, "if we could just live our religion without arguing about it!"

Well, it certainly would. And it's not only church officials who are guilty of this. There are too many families where religion begins with formal churchgoing, hymn singing, Bible reading, or other strictly ecclesiastical activities . . . and that's where it ends.

Don't misunderstand me. I know that all these things are important and necessary ingredients in religious faith. But I also think that religion should be simply *lived* as a part of everyday life. It should come to the rescue of people who need help. It should soften all judgments with tolerance and compassion. It should help all members of the family over the hurdles and roadblocks they encounter.

Teaching it to children should be a natural, effortless thing. I remember once when Elizabeth came home from school in tears. Some schoolmate whom she considered her friend had been mean to her—or so she said. She was through with Becky, she sobbed. She'd never speak to her or play with her again. She went on and on, pouring out her resentment and anger.

Finally I said to her, "What do you know about Becky's home life?"

She admitted that she knew little or nothing about it.

"Well," I said, "I happen to know that it's not a very happy one. Becky's parents were divorced. Her mother has married again, and Becky doesn't get along with her stepfather. Her real father, whom she loves, never comes to see her. She's an unhappy, confused little girl. Maybe she did act badly toward you, but I don't think it's because she dislikes you. It's because there's great unhappiness and loneliness in her life. So try to be understanding, will you?"

"You mean she's taking it out on me," said Elizabeth, impressed and abashed. "I'll try, Mother, I'll try."

Just a simple little family scene, but I think it shows religion in action in daily life. *Judge not,* says the Bible. That was the lesson, and Elizabeth learned it.

In our family, we also believed in praying for one another in specific situations—and letting the person know we were doing it. Even in something as commonplace as school examinations, when one of the children would go off to face an important test, we'd say, "Well, we'll be praying for you." Or perhaps we'd simply say, "We'll be thinking of you." In our house, the words "thinking of you" are synonymous with "praying for you." Both Norman and I were convinced that if the children knew we were "thinking" about them at such times with love and concern, they derived a sense of comfort and reassurance that made good performance much easier.

Any parent can do this. It's a great way to bridge the generation gap. And it works both ways. Not long ago I was in Miami where I was supposed to give the keynote speech at a large convention. I had the usual pre-speech butterflies and tension. The night before the convention opened I called home to check on a few matters and Elizabeth came on the wire. "When do you give your talk tomorrow?" she asked.

"In the morning," I told her.

"Yes, but exactly what time will that be?"

That was all she said. But I knew that she would be thinking of (praying for) me at that precise moment. And I knew that all the times I had prayed for her in examination periods and other situations had been very real and vital experiences of God's presence in her life. That simple question of Elizabeth's proved to be one of the greatest spiritual moments of my life.

Religion is really love in action. It's caring, really caring, about what another person feels, or says, or is. You don't even have to know the person. Last Christmas a married couple we know took their small children to a store, gave them each some money, and told them to pick out something for a poor child their own age, to select it with care because it might be the only present the poor child received. The children were interested at once. Gravely, intently, they went about the business of picking out a gift for an unknown child. Nobody quoted the Golden Rule to them, but they were following it, and their reward was happiness.

When people really live their religion there is every probability that it will rub off on those around them. There was the case of David and Donna Hamilton, two friends of ours who have a Christian marriage in the sense that Christ makes all the major decisions in their life. When there is a dilemma or a problem, they simply turn to Him and ask for help and guidance . . . and they will tell you with absolute assurance that He never lets them down.

There was the time, for example, when they needed a house close enough to Boston for David to commute to a new job that he had taken. They asked the Lord to help them find a house, and they found one in what seemed to be a pleasant suburb. So they bought it. But as they became acquainted with their neighbors, it began to seem that it was not such a pleasant suburb after all. There was a lot of drinking. There was a lot of extramarital sex. No one ever went to church or had the slightest interest in religion. At neighborhood parties the favorite pastime seemed to be telling dirty jokes.

David and Donna were deeply troubled, but as newcomers they felt hesitant about making their own feelings and attitudes known. Then one night, after attending a party where the storytelling had been particularly loathsome, Donna decided to pray about it. "Lord," she said, "these are all intelligent, well-educated people. Why can't they ever talk about something worthwhile? Why do they have to tell these foul stories? What can we do?"

The answer she got, Donna says, strengthened her conviction that the Lord has a sense of humor. The answer was, "Why don't you try introducing some *clean* funny stories?"

So Donna and David assembled some clean funny stories, and at the next party they told one or two. The results were surprising. "You know," one man said, "it's a relief to laugh at something that isn't dirty for a change. Kind of refreshing, isn't it?"

"That's right," said one of the women. "To tell you the truth, I never did like telling dirty stories so much. But it seemed the thing to do."

So the dirty stories stopped. Then one day a neighbor asked David and Donna where they went every Sunday. "You just seem to vanish," he said.

That gave Donna her opening. "We drive in to Boston," she said, "and go to church. We wouldn't miss it for anything."

"Is that so?" said the neighbor, surprised. "Well, what exactly do you get out of it?"

Quietly, but eloquently and sincerely, David and Donna told him what they got out of it. "I'd like to know more about that," said the man. "And I know a couple of others around here who would too."

As a result, a little group began meeting in the Hamilton home. It grew larger as the word got around that here was something a lot more stimulating than cocktail parties, and a lot longer lasting. The excessive drinking in the community began to diminish. The furtive affairs and liaisons became less common. People began to blow the dust off their morals and their values. Within a year, that community was completely changed—all because two people who really lived their religion shared it with people who had none—and who were hungrier for it than they knew.

Religion—let's stop talking about it, let's stop arguing about it, let's stop analyzing it. Let's just try making it an integral part of the adventure of being a wife.

22

YOUR HUSBAND'S BEST BUSINESS CONSULTANT—YOU

One complaint that I hear all the time from discontented wives is that their husbands are too wrapped up in business affairs to pay much attention to them. "My husband comes home every night from the office with a brief-case full of papers. All he does is work. I might as well not be there." Or, "My husband is always going on business trips without me. Sometimes I feel more like a widow than a wife."

To such wives I often feel like saying, "If his work is the most important thing in your husband's life, learn to take an interest in it. Urge him to talk to you about it. Instead of resenting it, try to be a part of it."

I'm sure the instant reaction of some women would be: "But I have no business background, no specialized knowledge of my husband's job."

To this I would reply, "That doesn't matter. What you do have is specialized knowledge of your husband himself. You know—or should know—how he reacts to things, whether he tends to be too optimistic or too pessimistic, whether he's too bold or too timid, whether he resents authority or welcomes it, whether he's steady or panicky in a tense situation.

"Very often all you have to do to help him is *listen* intelligently when he talks about his work. Most men have a desperate need for someone in whom they can confide with complete assurance, absolute trust. Many jobs, especially jobs in big corporations, are so fiercely competitive that very often there is no such person in a man's working world. If, as a wife, you can be an always-trustworthy, always-available sounding board, you'll be making an enormous contribution to your husband's career."

A woman may also find, if she forces herself to take an interest in her husband's work, that she has more aptitude for business than she thinks. It never occurred to me, before I was married, that I would end up handling all the financial and tax matters in our family. But it soon became apparent to me that if Norman tried to balance checkbooks or started worrying about mortgages or domestic money matters, his creativity would simply dry up. I took over these chores, at first, mainly to relieve him of this burden. But then I found that I really enjoyed working with figures and budgets and so on. It was fun to use all the training in mathematics that I had had in school and college. What was a nightmare to Norman became a source of satisfaction to me.

Sometimes a woman who makes such an effort will develop into a real executive. Norman and I once had a friend named Charles Ulrich Bay, a very wealthy oilman and shipowner who at one time was the American ambassador to Norway. He also owned the well-known financial firm of Kidder, Peabody, & Co. His wife Josephine was a clearminded, intelligent woman—and her tycoon husband used her constantly as a sounding board. "Here's a business proposition that seems pretty good to me," he'd say to her. "Now, I want you to argue against it. Tell me what's wrong with it. Poke holes in it. Play the devil's advocate. Go ahead. Convince me that it's no good."

"But I don't know enough about it," Josephine would object.

"Telephone the office," he would retort. "Have them send you all the facts, all the statistics, all the reports. Learn everything you can about it today, and we'll discuss it again tonight."

For years this challenging give-and-take went on. Then Mr. Bay died. Norman was asked to conduct the funeral, and he did. We rode back from Woodlawn Cemetery in the car with the widow. She was bearing up bravely, but did not try to hide the depth of her grief or the extent of her loss. "I don't know how I'm going to live without him," she kept saying. "I just don't know what I'm going to do."

"Josephine," Norman said gently, "I know what Rick would want you to do. He'd want you to take over his work, take charge of everything yourself. Don't you realize that all these years he's been training you to do just that? Nobody knows as much about all his enterprises as you do. If ever a man taught his wife how to get along without him, he did."

"Do you really believe," she said slowly, "that I have what it takes to step into his shoes?"

"I believe it," Norman said. "What's more, your husband believed it. So why don't you make up your mind to do it—and do it!"

Josephine Bay did make up her mind, and she did do it. She became the first woman president of the big financial house of Kidder, Peabody, & Co., and president of the American Export Lines. She became, in the opinion of many experts, the greatest businesswoman in the United States. And it all began during those quiet hours in her own home when she made herself into a willing sounding board for her man.

Taking an interest in your husband's work is just one more way of making yourself indispensable to him. When Norman preaches his first sermon on Sunday mornings, I listen as critically and intelligently as I can. If there is some change of emphasis that I think would help, or some point that could be made clearer, I tell him about it in his office between services. Then, if he agrees, he can incorporate it when he preaches the same sermon at the second service. I read all his writings and try to offer constructive suggestions. The truth is, neither of us makes any major move or decision without consulting the other. The result is a closeness and a harmony that have grown steadily deeper through the years.

Also, I often accompany him on speaking trips which, between Sundays, may take us to the West Coast and stops in-between. He speaks at many national business conventions ranging all the way from the American Feed Manufacturers to the National Association of Retail Druggists to the National Selected Morticians. Also, he appears before many large gatherings of sales personnel. He constantly consults with me regarding his approach. We plan his speeches together, though he makes all final decisions.

Ours is a partnership that will last as long as we live—and both of us are confident that it will continue unchanged after the transformation known as death. Without that conviction, the future would be hard to face. But we have it, strong and unshakable.

I remember the time the great industrialist Alfred P. Sloan came to see Norman. He was president of General Motors, forceful, brilliant, tough, one of the most powerful men in the world. But he was lost, stunned, bewildered as a small boy because his wife of fifty-five years had died. "Dr. Peale," he said, "I have come to you with a question, and I want an unequivocal answer: yes or no. I have asked this question of other clergymen, but I have had only hesitant or evasive replies. The question is this: When I die, will I see my wife again? Answer me: yes or no."

Norman said to him, "Mr. Sloan, the answer to your question is yes. Absolutely and emphastically yes. I'm sure your wife was a good person. I'm sure the Lord, who loves her, has prepared a place for her where she is waiting for you. I am absolutely positive that you will see your wife again!"

Mr. Sloan drew a long sigh of relief. He sat there for a long time, talking about his wife, the bonds there had been between them, the comradeship he had known with her. She was the one, he said, who shared his early struggles in the automotive industry, the one who encouraged him when he was low, who took him down a peg or two when he got too cocky. She was the best business advisor he'd had. For more than half a century, she was the one he always turned to when he had a major decision to make. She was absolutely indispensable, he said. He didn't see how he could live or function without her.

"Mr. Sloan," said Norman, "you're not living without her. She's still with you, even though you can't see her. As time goes by, you will become more and more conscious of her loving concern surrounding you. The veil that separates us from our loved ones who have died is very thin. Some day you will walk through that veil yourself, and be with her forever."

Mr. Sloan accepted the answer that Norman gave him. He became calm and reassured, confident that some day he would see his "best business advisor" again. And I'm sure that when the time came for him to walk through the veil she was right there, waiting for him, on the other side.

❧ 23 ❧

A FEW KIND
WORDS FOR
FEMININITY

❧ The other day Norman and I were taking a plane from Newark. Sitting near us in the big air terminal was another couple. The man was a gentle-looking person with an air of patient resignation. The woman, who wore slacks and had her hair cut severely short, was as positive and assertive as her husband was meek and retiring. She was the one who tipped the porter, who carried the tickets, who strode up to the desk to ask for flight information. She spoke in a loud, authoritative voice. Her gestures were commanding and decisive. We watched this oddly matched pair with fascination until their plane was called and they disappeared from view.

"Do you suppose," Norman said, "she's one of those militant feminists who go around putting stickers on advertisements they don't like saying 'Unfair to women?'"

"Well," I said cautiously, "I don't know about that. But it's easy to see who runs the show in *that* marriage."

"I don't understand it," my husband said. "Of course, I don't understand quite a few things, but what I *really* don't understand is what's so good about a masculine woman or a feminine man!"

I'll have to agree with my husband. If the good Lord chose to divide the human race into two distinctive sexes,

234

I don't see why anyone should try to blur the distinction. It seems to me that a man should possess—and occasionally display—the basic characteristics of the male animal: aggressiveness, combativeness, a drive to be dominant in most areas, including marriage. I also think that unless a woman is willing to look and act and be feminine, she's never going to be a success as a wife or a mother or even as a person.

Sometimes I think European women understand this better than American wives do. Recently I read an interview with Madame Louis Jourdan, wife of the French movie star. She was talking to Eugenia Sheppard of the New York *Post* about marriage and the contrast in attitudes here and abroad. Said Madame Jourdan: "The way a French woman treats her husband is different. You cater to him all the time. He's the head of the family. We French women enjoy being wives and not competing. American women are very independent. I admire them, but we don't want to be that way."

Why don't they want to be that way? Because they value their femininity too much; their femininity and the rewards it brings them.

Madame Jourdan had some other interesting things to say. "Living with an actor is an everyday job. It means listening when his mood is high and talking when it's low. You are a slave to moods, but it's never dull. It's either heaven or a headache."

I must say, that view doesn't apply only to actors. There's one minister I know who fits that description very nicely!

Here's Madame Jourdan's formula for a long marriage . . . and she's talking to other wives: "*You have to keep making it attractive.*" What a lot of wisdom packed into just seven words! Madame Jourdan is saying that marriage is something you can never take for granted. It's not a machine that will run along predictably and accurately, like a clock. The variables are always changing. You have to keep working, adjusting, changing with them. If you don't, you are lost.

Of course, feminists would object to the implication that making a marriage work is primarily the woman's responsibility. But on the deepest level it really is. Since the human race began, woman's elemental role has been to attract and hold a mate. There are many other roles that she can and does play, but this one is basic.

I agree with the feminists in some things, such as their claim that women should receive equal pay for doing the same job as men, and have equal opportunity for advancement in any field.

But I can't go along with some of their more strident demands because it seems to me that instead of viewing the male-female relationship as complementary and mutually supportive, they regard it as a competitive struggle.

When women vociferously clamor for the right to compete with men, they become essentially combative—which is a masculine trait. They may insist on doing everything that men do, but inevitably in the process they become more like men. And obviously the more masculine they are, the less feminine they can be.

The trend away from femininity in this country is nothing new; it has been going on for years. Most of the change has come about during my lifetime. I think it really got under way after the first World War, when along with the right to vote women also insisted they had the "right" to drink, smoke, swear, and put aside standards of sexual conduct that they had maintained for generations. This drastic change in values was very apparent by the time I got to college, and it has been accelerating ever since.

Whether or not this "emancipation" of women had anything to do with the subsequent appearance of ugly manifestations in our society—the decline of everyday honesty, the increase in crime, the sexual permissiveness, the erosion of discipline, the disrespect for law, the contempt for authority, the increasing reliance on violence as a solution to problems—is something that can't be proved. But to me it seems highly probable that there is a direct connection.

Take a sensitive and intuitive genius like Irving Berlin: What is he saying when he writes a song with words as nostalgic and wistful as these?

> The girl that I marry will have to be
> As soft and pink as a nursery.

Is he just sketching a lacy and impossibly romantic Valentine, or is he trying to remind us of the days when America was stronger and better because its women had an identity and an integrity and an appeal that has been lost?

Along with this flight from femininity (and perhaps because of it) has come a corresponding feminization of men. Certainly in terms of dress and appearance the difference between the sexes has steadily diminished. The other day I saw a cartoon in which, having just married a shaggy couple, the minister was saying plaintively, "Now will one of you please kiss the bride?" Funny? Well, yes. But also a little depressing. The more alike the sexes become, the less exciting relationships between them are bound to be.

This whole trend works against the powerful polarity that is built into sex differentiation, the force that makes male-female attraction the deep and thrilling thing that it ought to be and can be. Not long ago I was with a group of young women where this subject of feminine liberation came up. "Men," said one of them scornfully, "don't want us to be their equals. Look at the way women are portrayed in a magazine like *Playboy*—mindless, brainless objects for sexual gratification, nothing more. It's time we put an end to this sort of exploitation. Who wants to be just a plaything for some man?"

Well, no one wants to be just a plaything, I agree. But what sort of sexual partner is a woman going to make if this kind of negative thought, this sense of grievance and resentment, is uppermost in her mind? Noncooperative, at best. Downright frigid, at worst. If, indeed, with such a hostile attitude she's able to attract a man at all!

I don't pretend for a moment that the lavender-and-lace type of woman portrayed by Mr. Berlin could come back and function successfully in today's streamlined world. That dreamgirl is gone for good. But if modern women are wise, they will make a conscious and deliberate effort to retain some of her qualities: the gentleness, the compassion, the idealism, yes, the purity that men once expected from their wives—and still hope for and still need, whether they admit it or not.

Meantime, to all militant feminists, I would just say this: Ladies, your real enemy in your search for happiness is not masculine prejudice, or masculine exploitation, or masculine anything. Your real enemy is the lack of femininity in you.

❧ 24 ❧

HELP YOUR
CHILD TO
GOOD MANNERS

❧ One of the best friends Norman and I ever had was Dr. Smiley Blanton, the eminent psychiatrist. He was the expert Norman approached many years ago when he needed help in dealing with some of the deep emotional maladjustments of people who came to him for pastoral counseling. Out of that minister-psychiatrist team effort grew the great American Foundation of Religion and Psychiatry that helps so many thousands of confused and unhappy people today.

Smiley had uncanny insight into all sorts of human problems, but especially the problems of children. Children fascinated him, and Smiley fascinated them. He seemed to understand their thought-processes and actions in a very special way.

For example, when our son John was a baby, he took his time about learning to talk. His older sister Margaret began to talk early and never stopped. But John remained silent well past the age when most babies begin to use words. He stayed speechless for so long that we became worried and asked Smiley to help us. Smiley observed the situation for a little while, then handed down a reassuring verdict. Nothing was wrong with John. His older sister talked so much that John simply felt no need to say anything. If we just separated the two for a few days, Smiley said, John would begin to speak for himself. Somewhat dubious, we tried it. Sure enough, John began talking at once and has been highly articulate ever since.

Years ago, when our children were still quite small, I had a conversation with Smiley that made quite an impression on me. He and I were sitting in a car outside a department store, waiting for his wife, Margaret, who was doing some last-minute Christmas shopping. Customers were streaming out, laden with parcels, when a stocky, red-faced woman with two children approached the entrance. She didn't wait for the doorway to be clear. She barged straight in, stepping on toes, jostling the parcel-laden shoppers, clearing a path like a bulldozer for herself and the children.

"That woman," Smiley said thoughtfully, "is a thief."

"You mean, she's a shoplifter?" I asked, astonished.

"No," he said, "nothing like that. But she's robbing her children of something more important than anything in any store. She's making it impossible for them to learn good manners. And by so doing she may well be ruining their lives."

I protested that this judgment seemed a bit harsh.

"No," he insisted, "it isn't. Do you realize that about eighty percent of the problems I'm called on to deal with professionally would never have arisen if the people in their formative years had been taught to have manners—really good manners?"

"That's hard to believe," I objected.

"Look," said the old doctor, "life's a series of red and green lights, isn't it? A child who's been taught good manners knows what's expected of him in a given situation. As a result, he tends to be confident and serene. But a child with no manners, or bad manners, is bewildered and lost. He keeps making mistakes, and the mistakes make him feel unpopular and rejected. These are the people who wind up in my office: insecure, self-centered, unable to give love or receive it because they were never taught to be considerate of other people. They can't play the game of life because they don't know the rules. I hope you'll remember this where your own children are concerned."

"I hope so too," I said fervently.

Actually, if I do say so myself, I think Norman and I did succeed in raising three reasonably well-mannered children. One reason, I'm sure, was that we both instinctively agreed with Smiley about the importance of good manners. Another, no doubt, was that as a minister's family we were often on display and supposed to act as a good example. Then, too, more than in most families, our children traveled with us, had to eat with us in public places, and so on. To some extent, they lived in an adult world and had to display adult behavior.

In trying to teach them good manners, though, we did work out a few principles to go by. "Courtesy," someone once said, "is love in small things." Here are a few of the rules we found helpful in liberating and strengthening this kind of love in our children.

First, and most important, you've got to give them a good model to imitate. Children are like mirrors; they reflect whatever's held up in front of them. Why should a boy hold a door open for his mother if his father doesn't? Why shouldn't a girl interrupt somebody in mid-sentence if that's what her mother does? Before you can hope to teach manners, you have to mind your *own* manners.

Next, whenever possible, show them the same courtesy that you'd use in dealing with an adult. Parents sometimes have to give orders, and not all of them can be in the form of polite requests. But an occasional "please" or "thank you" or "excuse me" addressed to a small child will make him begin to realize that good manners can sometimes benefit *him*, that they're two-way streets, not just a set of unreasonable rules imposed on him by tyrannical grown-ups.

Third, encourage them to like people. If a child can be made to feel that the world is a welcoming place where people are more likely to help than hinder him, he will tend to be outgoing and friendly, and good manners will come to him much more readily than if he is suspicious or hostile.

Most small children are naturally friendly, but this trusting attitude can be damaged by well-meaning parents. I think it's always a mistake, for instance, to force children into activities that may make them self-conscious or ill-at-ease. More than once I've heard Norman recall the agonies he suffered as a sensitive child when summoned by his admiring parents to recite poetry to guests. It reached the point where, if he heard a knock on the front door, he would run and hide in the attic. In the end, by sheer will-power, he taught himself to speak effectively. But he admits that to this day he can still feel shy and self-conscious with strangers when he meets them individually or in small groups.

A fourth thing we tried to do was to put emphasis on things involving true considerateness, not just stock phrases or gestures. You can teach a child to say, "Pleased to meet you," or "Thank you for a nice time," but you can also teach such phrases to a parrot. To give up a toy to someone less privileged, to let another child have first turn because he's a guest, to keep quiet because someone is ill or resting or working—these voluntary acts of thoughtfulness are much closer to the heart of good manners. And when children begin to admire this sort of behavior in others (as eventually they will), then the battle is almost won.

The last principle we tried to keep in mind—and again this was Dr. Blanton's idea—was not to expect too much too soon. The capacity for good manners grows as the child grows; you can encourage it, but you can't hurry it beyond a certain point. You can't expect a two- or three-year-old to share his playthings gladly. You have to remember that a four-year-old's fantastic tales aren't really lies; they're just a friendly effort to share some fascinating ideas. If a six-year-old becomes loud and aggressive, you can curb his rudeness, but it also helps to remember that he is trying to achieve a degree of independence and handle a few life-situations for himself. Each age has its capacities and its limitations. Too-great expectations on the part of the parents can make everybody miserable.

I think parents also have to resign themselves to the fact that a child is going to act differently in different surroundings. But this isn't limited to children. On Art Linkletter's show, a baffled mother once asked him about this. "Why," she said, "does my little boy behave so much better outside our house than in it?"

"Madam," replied Art Linkletter, "don't you?"

I wish I could say that I thought good manners among children were on the increase in this country. But I can't say that I do. You see too many uncontrolled and undisciplined youngsters. You hear too many surly teen-agers snarling and snapping at their parents. You see too many street scenes where mothers, goaded beyond endurance, are screaming like fishwives at their children—always a mistake, because what a rude child really wants is for someone to make him behave; the last thing he wants is to be confronted by an adult who is ruder than he is.

I suppose it's all part of the rebellion against authority that in recent years has become so prevalent in our society. But it has to be counteracted somehow, somewhere, if our children are to grow up to be stable, balanced, problem-solving citizens in a world where the problems seem to grow larger every day.

There's only one institution that can reverse the trend:

🌿 25 🌿

A DIFFICULT
MARRIAGE
PROBLEM

🌿 People sometimes ask me, "What is the most difficult problem in human relations that you and your husband are called upon to solve?" I'm not sure that I can give a final answer, but certainly one of the most common is the marriage that's in jeopardy because one of the partners is being or has been unfaithful to the other.

Let me make this clear right at the start: I have no sympathy for adulterers. I have no patience with the sophisticates who condone or excuse infidelity on the grounds of "situation ethics" or any other consideration. To me, the married partner who is unfaithful is breaking the laws of God and man. It is never justified. It is always sinful, always immoral, always wrong.

I know that a great deal of infidelity exists in our society. But I also think that to some extent it has been overplayed. I know there are men who chase women in order to bolster a shaky ego or to reassure themselves about a doubtful masculinity. And there are women who drift from one affair to another in an effort to fill some deep psychological void within themselves. But I think that men are mostly monogamous—and women are too. I believe the typical hardworking, decent American (or Briton, or Spaniard, or Filipino, for that matter) would rather limit himself to one sex partner, a wife whom he loves, than not. Infidelity is not natural for him: it's unnatural; it's immoral.

It's unnatural and immoral for his wife, too. Something deep inside the average woman fears infidelity and flinches from it. What she feels is not fear of the possible consequences so much as the fear of self-condemnation, self-disgust. That is to say, her soul, her spiritual self, reacts against immorality. Love, wifehood, goodness, are built into her by the Creator. I once heard of an unfaithful wife who came home late one afternoon after spending a couple of hours in some hotel room with her lover. She looked through the window of her own living room and saw her husband sitting on the floor by the fire, playing checkers with their little boy, waiting for her to come home. And the pang of guilt and shame and misery that this woman felt was so acute, so profound, so painful, that in that instant, in her mind, she abandoned her lover and her love affair and never went back to them. It always seemed to me that that was a true portrayal of the basic feminine reaction to adultery.

As for the average husband, he knows perfectly well that extramarital sex is usually an unsatisfactory and furtive business where the momentary thrill is not worth the risk, the trouble, the emotional (and sometimes the financial) investment. Presumably he has worked hard for a number of years to build a home, raise a family, establish a place for himself in a society which, however permissive it has become, still has certain standards and certain rules. Why jeopardize all that for a little short-term excitement? The price tag is too high, unless—and this is the key point—unless something is seriously wrong with his married life, unless there is some unfilled emotional vacuum, unless there is some deep anger or resentment that is demanding this form of retaliation.

In other words, when a husband or a wife jumps out of

the corral, one way or another they have been goaded or prodded into making the leap.

I believe that there are thousands of homes—maybe millions—where the seeds of infidelity exist in the form of irritations, maladjustments, small areas of disagreement that can—unless something is done about them—grow into a tangle of weeds that can choke any marriage. I'm convinced that when infidelity has become an imminent threat or an actuality in a marriage, it's because nobody recognized these warning signs, nobody dealt with these early symptoms, nobody took an emotional inventory that might have made changes and remedies possible while there was still time.

People think that it's the big, drastic things that destroy marriage, and I'll admit it usually looks that way. But it's really the little things that cause the big things. A woman may divorce her husband because she learns that he's sleeping with his secretary, or is keeping a whole harem of mistresses. But if she could trace the causality back far enough, she might discover that it all began because she couldn't be bothered to put the cap back on the toothpaste—even though she knew that capless toothpaste tubes drove her husband crazy.

Just the other day a woman from out of town whom I know slightly came up to me and started complaining bitterly because her husband had stopped escorting her to church. They had been married for twenty years, she said, and her husband had always gone to church with her. Now, suddenly, he refused to go any more. She said she thought he had lost his mind, and it was obvious that she wanted me to think so too—and agree with her so that she could relay this confirmation without delay to her mindless mate.

"Does he tell you why he won't go?" I asked.

"No," she snapped. "He has no reason. He just won't go."

"Well," I said, "he must have some reason. Perhaps the

minister did or said something that offended him." (This is the first thing a minister's wife thinks of!)

"No," she said. "He has no reason. He's just doing it to annoy me! He knows I don't like to sit by myself in church. So that's why he won't go."

That's why *you're* annoyed, I thought, because things aren't the way *you* want them. Aloud I said mildly, "Have you told him this?"

"Of course," she said. "I tell him all the time!"

"Since you've asked for my advice," I said, "I'll give it to you. Stop nagging your husband about this. Go to church alone, or with a friend. Pray to understand your husband better and to be able to communicate with him better. Try putting into practice the religious principles you learn at church. In other words, be patient and tolerant and kind. Stop thinking about yourself. Try thinking about your husband. If you do, I'm sure you'll be back together, in church and everywhere else. If you don't, I think you'll find yourself without an escort more and more often."

Time and time again Norman and I have seen a marriage go on the rocks because one partner was determined to change the other—and the other could not change. I remember one couple in particular where the wife was the dissatisfied one. She was a rather ambitious person who wanted a heaping measure of the so-called good things of life: money, clothes, cars, travel, social position, and so on. Her husband, who sold real estate, was an easygoing person. He saw no reason to work twelve hours a day when he could get by with six. He was happier puttering around in his basement workshop than having dinner at the country club. He had two or three close friends, and that was good enough for him. He didn't care whether his activities were reported on the society page of the newspaper or not.

For years this wife kept hounding her husband to work harder, make more money, amount to something. When he refused to do all these things, she began to complain more and more to anyone who would listen to her. Quite often this included Norman and me, because she knew her husband admired Norman, and she thought that if Norman backed up her criticism it might have some effect.

One day, I remember, she was listing her husband's deficiencies to Norman with even more vehemence than usual. Not only was Fred lazy, she said, but he was sloppy. He was untidy. He spilled pipe tobacco and ashes on everything. And not only that, he drank too much. He was turning into a real alcoholic.

At this, my usually patient husband spoke up rather loudly. "Marilyn," he said, "I know Fred pretty well. He may not be a man who's going to set the world on fire, and he may spill ashes occasionally, but he is not a boor and he's not an alcoholic. He is a good husband and a good provider. At least, he has been so far. But I don't think he will be much longer, because you are going to drive him away. He wants a quiet, peaceful home. No man can stand the kind of criticism and disapproval that you're handing out. You're going to break up your marriage by insisting on change just because you want things the way you want them."

"He'd never break up our marriage," said Marilyn angrily.

"You're the one," Norman told her, "who's breaking up the marriage. What's more, you're the one who is going to suffer most when it is broken. Fred will go right on having his work and his hobbies and his friends. But what will you have? Not much! I can see you right now, old and lonely and bitter. And you'll still be blaming Fred—for not being something he never was!"

What happened to that marriage? Exactly what Norman predicted. It did break up. We still see them, separately, from time to time. Fred is by himself, but he actually seems a happier person. Marilyn, who never remarried, is lonely and bitter. And it was all so unnecessary! What Marilyn needed was not a go-getter husband, or more money, or more glamor in her life. What she needed was the determination to make her marriage work, using the raw materials that were available. But she never did this. And so the marriage died.

The sad and ironic thing is that I'm sure Marilyn could have brought about some of the changes she so ardently desired. Not fundamental personality changes in her husband, perhaps, but surely some of the lesser ones. Pipe ashes, for example. If she had told Fred, quietly and lovingly, that this was something that did upset her, something that it was within his power to correct, he might have listened to her. If perhaps in exchange she had offered to stop doing something in the same category, change some small habit of her own that annoyed him, I'm sure he would have made the necessary effort.

I heard, once, of a marriage counselor in Honolulu who always urges a quarreling couple to write down their pet peeves about each other. He studies each list. Then he draws up a contract for the couple to sign, a contract that will last for a week. If the wife will agree to cut down her cigarettes to ten per day, the husband will help her with the dishes three nights a week. If he will talk to her at breakfast instead of reading the paper, she will stop wearing curlers in her hair. That sort of thing. At the end of the week he calls them in. If they have honored the contract, it remains in force and some new, carefully balanced conditions are added. Apparently this give-and-take technique has been effective in saving a lot of marriages.

I realize that the points I've been trying to make in this chapter are simple and that they've been made before. But I think they're worth repeating to anyone—especially any woman—who wants a marriage to work.

Watch for the small areas of friction and try to eliminate

them before they can generate major centrifugal forces.

Don't expect perfection from the person you married, because you can't offer it yourself.

Try to control your own ego, at least to the point of seeing both sides of any controversy or disagreement.

Study your man and try to supply his basic emotional needs.

If you can do these things, the spectre of infidelity need never cast a shadow across the adventure of being a wife.

❧ 26 ❧

SPEND A DAY
OR TWO
WITH ME

❧ The bedside clock said six-thirty A.M.

We were in our farmhouse on Quaker Hill at Pawling, New York, where we spend some of our days doing creative work and writing. It was a beautiful morning and I was wide-awake. There are "slow starters" and "fast starters," and I'm one of the latter. Early in our marriage this was an area that needed patience and understanding if friction was to be avoided, for Norman starts slowly, although he surely does get going later. He does some of his best creative work late at night, when I have long since given up! On the other hand, my mind needs the freshness of morning, the clarity that comes from being uncluttered.

So, quietly, I got up. I could spend at least forty-five minutes at the task of turning some of Norman's recorded sermons into printed form. Each month three of these printed sermons are mailed to over 600,000 people all over the United States and in 111 countries around the world. Anyone who wishes to receive them may write to the Foundation for Christian Living, Pawling, New York, 12564.

I love working for the Foundation, because I really consider it my brainchild. I think every wife needs some area where she can feel that she is building and developing something on her own . . . and this is mine.

Getting these sermons ready for mailing is a tricky business, because Norman speaks and preaches without a manuscript. He prepares a careful outline, which he memorizes, but from that point on everything is extemporaneous. Since he preaches two almost but not quite identical sermons each Sunday morning, I always have two transcriptions to work with. Blending them into one smooth-flowing manuscript is a challenging business.

Picking up the manuscript I had worked on the evening before, sure enough, I found some sentences that could be improved. What sounds great as the spoken word is sometimes slow and wordy when read. My husband gives me a free hand in editing, and since no one has heard him preach more sermons than I (I go to both identical morning services every Sunday), the final result, hopefully, is Norman in writing instead of speaking.

At seven-thirty A.M. the editing is done. Now there is time to start the clothes washer before getting breakfast. By eight o'clock I had brought the percolator to our upstairs sitting room and plugged it in. I found Norman down the hall exercising vigorously on the exercycle on which he works out daily.

"Breakfast will be ready in fifteen minutes," I said.

"That's good. What are we going to have?"

"Bacon and eggs. Is that all right?"

"Sounds great. And that coffee cake. But be sure to heat it."

We had a leisurely breakfast. Fortunately I could put the clothes in the dryer before bringing the breakfast upstairs, so my morning was off to a good start.

We planned the day over a second cup of coffee and also discussed some pending decisions. What about that requested speaking engagement out West? Could it be tied in with that business association convention in Chicago? Also, the final editing of Norman's weekly newspaper column was due. He writes for some hundred and fifty papers.

The telephone bell rang. It was our daughter Elizabeth who lives one-half mile away. Her usual morning call is one we always anticipate. After the customary catching up on news, she hesitantly asked, "What are you doing right after lunch, Mother?"

I knew what was coming, so I gulped and said brightly, "Oh, nothing of any importance if I can help you. Do you want me to baby-sit?"

"Oh, that would be great! And I will only be gone about an hour and a half. How about one-thirty?"

"I'll be there," and we discussed a new recipe she had used at dinner the night before. My best new dishes always come from my daughters.

By nine-thirty Norman and I were both ready to leave for the office in Pawling—breakfast dishes washed, beds made, clothes from the dryer folded and put away or in the ironing basket in the basement, the sandwich lunch I had made for myself (Norman was going to Rotary) and my briefcase in the car. After settling an outside repair job with our caretaker, we were ready to go.

Before leaving for the office each day I stand in the doorway of each room in the house for a quick look. Is anything out of order? I put a chair in place here, discard a newspaper there, return records to the hi-fi cabinet in the family room, water the plants, inspect the powder room, etc., etc. All this may sound fussy, but it is the easiest way for me to fulfill what I consider my first responsibility, that of being a wife and the kind of housekeeper my husband appreciates and needs so that he can be free from any irritation that detracts from his creativity. I, personally, do not need this kind of perfection in a house. If I put it in order two or three times a week, it would be enough and the slight clutter wouldn't bother me. But I have trained myself to do it the other way. Frankly, though, it isn't any easier after all these years of married life. I still resist and even resent it a bit, but do it because it helps to make a happy and peaceful home. My goal has always been to be as intelligent and hard-working about my home as about the fulfillment of my career. And my home always comes first.

Off to the office, four miles away. We take separate cars because I mustn't forget my baby-sitting job! We have adjoining offices and share three secretaries who know that we work as a team. Norman starts writing and making phone calls; I go to a policy meeting in the conference room with the executives and supervisors. It lasts two hours, giving me time for some correspondence and phone calls and a quick lunch at my desk before joining my grandchildren.

Rebecca, age two and a half, is a lively, imaginative child, never still a minute, always investigating, interested in everything. Her sister, Katheryn, just over one year, is beginning to walk, although she still gets there faster on all fours. One hour and a half with these two is really fascinating and demands complete attention. It is a good thing for grandmothers to be reminded of what their daughters and daughters-in-law go through in bringing up a family. We have seven grandchildren, the greatest blessings of our lives.

Back at the office after my baby-sitting stint, I spend an hour dictating letters, interspersed with the usual interruptions including telephone calls. Once Norman called me into his office.

"Ruth," he said, "give me your thinking on a problem. It's really a honey. But first read this letter."

He busied himself with some papers until I had opportunity to read and think about the communication he handed me. It was from a woman in a distant state, one of Norman's avid readers who suddenly found herself in a crisis.

For some time her husband had been acting "strangely." He seemed under great tension. To all her inquiries he declared that nothing was wrong. But it was evident to the sharp eyes and keen intuition of the wife that something was undermining her husband's well-being. Finally he had broken down and confessed that he had been stealing from a big account. He had concealed this by a skillful manipulation of the figures. But he was sure that "someone was onto him" and he was living in mortal fear of exposure.

"But what have you done with the money you have taken? I've never seen anything more than the regular amounts," the wife asked. Despairingly, the husband confessed to ʳpeculations that went badly. He fully intended, so he said, to return the "principal" after he had made a profit.

ᵣ "So now," the wife asked us, "what do we do? We talked the matter over and agreed to ask your advice, and so great is our confidence in you that we will do exactly as you advise."

"Well, Ruth, what do you say to that one?" Norman asked.

"I don't just know," I replied, "but we know how to find the answer." We sat quietly for a few moments asking guidance for the couple in crisis. It is our belief, verified in hundreds of cases, that no matter how complex a matter may be, if Divine guidance is sincerely asked for it will be given.

"I'm going to get this man on the telephone," Norman said. And he did.

"We are working on your problem," he explained to the husband. "There are a couple of questions I want to ask. First, is another woman involved? Is that why you have been stealing?"

The man replied firmly in the negative.

"How much have you taken?"

"Over a period of ten years, about eighty thousand dollars."

"Whew," exclaimed Norman, "you're really in deep. How much money can you get together in a hurry?"

The husband calculated, then said, "Maybe fifteen thousand."

"Are you sorry enough, not only scared, but sorry enough to start being honest from now on?"

The unhappy man said he had brought himself to the point where he would "do anything for peace of mind."

"All right. I will telephone you in a little while after we go over it again."

Hanging up the receiver, Norman said, "Here's my prescription for this fellow. I just want to check it with you. It's this: That he take the fifteen thousand dollars he can rake up and with his wife go to his employer. He is to tell him the whole story, then turn over the money and say he will pay back the remainder with interest if it takes the rest of his life. And he must add that he deserves prosecution if they so desire. But he can hardly make money in prison to pay them back. In other words, he is to come clean and throw himself upon their mercy. If he doesn't do this, they will catch him anyway, in time. Meanwhile he is breaking up inside. The only question is how sincere he is. But that is up to his employers to decide."

Having agreed upon this procedure, Norman called him back and gave him our advice. Surprisingly, the man said, "I had thought of that myself but didn't have the nerve. But now that you tell me that it's the thing to do I shall do it at once. Even if they throw me in jail I'll at least have the satisfaction for once in my miserable life of being a real man."

An hour later a phone call came from the employer. "I understand that you are aware of our problem. The man came in with his shocking story, which we already suspected. We are going to accept his offer but put him to work at something where money management is not involved. I'd just like to ask one thing: Who got the idea of this honest confession and offer?"

"Oh, he thought of it, and we agreed with him," Norman said.

"Well," replied the other, "maybe he's more of a man than he has been acting. Anyway, we're taking a chance on him."

The office closes at four P.M., but Norman and I generally stay on for at least half an hour. The quiet of a deserted office seems to reduce the strain and sometimes I think I get more done then than all through the day.

The evening is spent at a dinner party in the home of friends, where we relax and have a good time.

The next day we leave our farm home early to go to New York City, seventy-five miles away. Norman has a staff meeting with the other ministers of the Marble Collegiate Church, and I will meet with some of the women leaders of the church to help plan a program scheduled six weeks ahead.

We go together for lunch with some friends from out of town who visit Marble Church at least twice a year and we always anticipate a visit with them.

After checking on domestic matters in our Fifth Avenue apartment (this is a manse belonging to the church), I go to our uptown office across the street. In addition to the office at the church at 29th and Fifth, we long ago felt it necessary to have an office away from the church and nearer home where we could be assured of a measure of privacy. Here two secretaries handle all Norman's appointments and speaking schedules, part of his enormous correspondence, and all his personal telephone calls. It is from this office that I fulfill my obligations connected with the many boards and committees on which I serve.

I recall that on one occasion as I entered the waiting room I noticed a well-dressed, middle-aged woman sitting there in an attitude of utmost despondency. It was obvious that she had been weeping. Despair was registered in every line of her face.

Nodding to her, I went on into the business office where Norman's secretary explained that this woman, a Mrs. Fredrickson, had come all the way from a midwestern city without an appointment to see Norman about her personal problem. But Norman had just left town on a series of speaking engagements.

It happened that I was due at the executive committee meeting of an important organization and was scheduled to preside. The meeting was set for two o'clock and it was now one-thirty, barely allowing time to get to the meeting. But my husband and I have always felt that human considerations come first. "Since my husband is not available, Mrs. Fredrickson, would you like to talk to me?" I asked.

"Oh, yes, Mrs. Peale," she replied. "I once heard you speak and I know how much Dr. Peale depends upon you. Please let me talk with you."

"Well," I replied, "the only way we can do this is for you to come with me in my car and we'll talk while driving to my meeting."

Thirty minutes were required to make the drive, and as soon as we started I asked her to tell me what was on her mind. Figuring the time at our disposal, I let her pour out her heart for a full twenty minutes without interrupting. I knew that a complete mental catharsis would not only make her feel better temporarily but also prepare the way for corrective measures that might follow.

Her problem was a husband suffering from obsessive fear and apprehension, which produced constant tension within him. These fears, which apparently stemmed from childhood, were wholly inexplicable to her. Her own makeup was a balanced one, and she had no background or training out of which might come insights into the complex nature of her husband's problem.

The unrelieved fear and tension had boiled up in her husband to the point where she could "take it no more."

Reaching our parking place, I turned off the motor and

said, "All right, now that is the problem; let's begin on the solution. And I suggest that you do the following: Say to yourself, (1) I have a problem and will face it creatively and courageously. (2) Others have had this same problem and have solved it. I can do the same. (3) I will study the proper procedures I should take and follow advice. (4) I will turn the problem over to God in complete faith that He will bring it out right."

Then I asked her to come into the building with me while I telephoned to the American Foundation of Religion and Psychiatry at 3 West 29th Street. This is the largest counseling service ever established involving psychiatrists and psychologists working together with clergymen of all faiths. It was organized in 1940 by Norman and the late Dr. Smiley Blanton. Its staff comprises men and women counselors expert and experienced in handling all human problems. Though their schedule is a heavy one, I persuaded the Director to make a place for Mrs. Fredrickson, who went immediately for a counseling session. From this she gained deeper understanding of herself and her husband. Later her husband accepted counseling and gained insights that relieved him of his inner conflicts.

Norman saw them both some time later and led them into a creative spiritual experience which gave new strength to their marriage. Apparently I was guided to handle this human problem satisfactorily, for things continue to go well with the Fredricksons. And, by the way, I made the meeting on time.

Six-thirty finds me back at Marble Church, where the dining hall is filled to capacity for a meeting of one of the clubs in the church. For years Norman did all the speaking at Marble Church and I limited my public speaking to outside groups. Then someone discovered that we were a team in this area, also. But it took many years before I was asked to speak in the pulpit (for just three minutes!) to give a laymen's report looking toward the raising of the budget.

Well, these are only highlights from a couple of typical days in my life. There are never enough hours in the day to do all the things I want to do. But I like life that is busy and demanding. Our days are full of hard work—we never stop. It may sound hectic, but actually it's fascinating. We wouldn't have it any other way.

❧ 27 ❧

ONE AFTERNOON
IN WINTER

❧ I'm finishing this book in the same place where I started it, our old white farmhouse on Quaker Hill in Pawling, New York. Inside the house, all is the same, except that now a fire is crackling on the hearth. Outside all is different: The soft greens of April have been replaced by the stark blacks and whites and grays of winter. Snow lies deep along our fence-rows, and the great maples lift their gaunt arms against the sky. At night the stars blaze above fields so quiet that you can hear the silence sing. December is a good time to finish things.

It seems like a long time since that dark-haired girl in the psychology class stood up to challenge my views on marriage. But I'm glad now that she did. I'm glad, too, that Norman encouraged and supported me in the writing of this book which is my answer to her and people like her. Without his help I could never have finished it.

I've found that by the time you're through with it, a book becomes something like an old friend, rewarding at times, demanding at others, cantankerous and difficult on bad days, fun and exciting on good ones. We have talked about this book and worked on it here at the farm, on innumerable two-hour drives into New York City, on short trips and on long transoceanic plane flights. We have made rough drafts in London and revised them in Madrid and

262

Rome. We have written sections in Holland, Michigan, and discarded them in Amsterdam, Holland. The final result, as I predicted to Norman, is rather like a patchwork quilt, but I hope the central idea and message have come through.

As I've indicated many times, my whole intent and purpose have been simply to affirm my faith in the ancient and honorable estate known as marriage, to try to answer some of the critics, to persuade some of the doubters and skeptics that, far from being a burden or a bore, it can be a great adventure. Like all true adventures, it has its risks and its hazards, but without these it *would* be a bore.

I have tried to convey, furthermore, my conviction that the success or failure of any marriage depends primarily on the wife. She is—or should be—the one who largely determines the emotional climate in which a marriage grows and flourishes—or withers and dies. Regardless of what the feminists may say or think, in our society the chief responsibility of most women is the creation and maintenance of a home. And the whole fabric of our culture is determined by how well or how badly they do the job.

In saying this, I certainly am not downgrading women; I am assigning to them the key role in civilization as we know it. Men may supply the energies that keep the ship of state moving forward. But women are the rudder—and the rudder determines where the ship will go.

I also hope I have managed to get across the importance of constant effort and study and compromise and adjustment if a marriage is to grow into the kind of relationship that I know it can be. In a way, marriage is like religion: it works when you work at it. A good marriage doesn't just happen; it has to be made to happen. But when you really work at it, and it really works, nothing in the world pays such dividends or brings such rewards.

Now that I'm at the end of the book, I keep thinking of

little episodes that I wish I had included; just the small, warm, wonderful moments of family living that are the dividends I'm talking about. Like the time, for instance, when our John was a little boy of seven or eight and had an accident in which his ear was cut very badly. We rushed him to the hospital where they put him on the operating table. In preparation, they emptied his pockets of all his boyish treasures: marbles and old candies and a pocket-knife and bits of string; I can see them to this day and still feel the tug at my heart.

He lay there, so pale and uncomplaining, while we held his hands, all smudged and dirty from playing. And Norman, thinking of all the times he had sent John away from the dinner table with orders to wash his hands, said suddenly —because the emotion he was feeling had to go somewhere —"John, I'll *never* make you go and wash your hands at mealtime again!"

Well, of course, the ear was patched up with no permanent damage, and the day finally came when John appeared at the dinner table unwashed. "John," said his father absently, "go and wash your hands." Whereupon John fixed him with a reproachful gaze. "You *promised!*" he said. I forget now what compromise we made, and perhaps the story has little significance for others, but it has a lot for me.

Or the time when I was in our New York apartment and Norman was filling a speaking engagement on the West Coast. At four in the morning my bedside telephone rang. Dazed with sleep, I picked it up and heard Norman's voice coming all the way from Seattle. "Ruth," he said, and I could tell he was upset, "are you all right?"

"All right?" I repeated numbly. "Why, yes. I'm fine."

"Are you *sure* you're fine?" insisted Norman. "Do you *really* feel all right?"

"Of course," I answered, now sitting bolt upright and wide-awake. "I feel great. What's the matter with you?"

It seemed that Norman had come back to the hotel after making his speech, had gone to sleep, and had had a nightmare in which I was terribly ill—in fact, dying. It had frightened him so that he had seized the phone and called me to make sure that it was only a dream.

We talked for a while, and I forget what else we said, but I'll never forget my husband's last words. "Ruth," he said, "you have the sweetest voice in the world . . ."

Once a man and a woman have attained this kind of closeness, it will last as long as they live. And longer. And this deep relationship comes to many people; people like our two friends, Jack and Virginia Kyle.

Let me end this book with their touching story. Jack Kyle was Chief Engineer of the New York Port Authority. One thousand engineers and technicians worked under him. Name almost any of the great engineering projects around New York City—the Lincoln Tunnel, the lower level of the George Washington Bridge, Kennedy, LaGuardia, and Newark airports, the beginning of the World Trade Center —all these were built under Jack's genius and guidance.

He and his wife were about as close as it is possible for a couple to be. Virginia was a gentle, very beautiful, highly intelligent woman. It was a terrible blow to all of us when she was stricken with cancer. The doctors said that nothing could be done, that it was just a matter of time.

Jack Kyle accepted the verdict with quiet resignation. "I don't know how I'll live without her," he said to Norman. "But we've had a wonderful life together. I'm grateful for that. If it's God's will that Virginia goes first, then His will be done."

In the hospital, Virginia Kyle's condition grew steadily worse. Her husband spent hours at her bedside. Then suddenly, with no warning, a heart attack struck Jack Kyle. He lingered a few days. Then a second attack took him suddenly; he was dead.

It was impossible to keep the truth from his wife; when her husband did not come to see her, she guessed—and no one had the heart to hide the sad fact from her. She asked quietly when the funeral was to be. When told that it was to be Sunday at the Marble Collegiate Church at two-thirty, she said that she was going to be there. In her condition, the doctor said that was impossible. But she would not accept this. She kept saying that she was going to be there.

One half hour before the funeral, Virginia Kyle died. And when Norman conducted the service for her husband, no one in the church had any doubts. Virginia Kyle had said she would be there. And she was.

Can you believe that for a woman like that death ended the adventure of being a wife? I don't think so. I think it was just the beginning.